*Railroads, Freight,
and Public Policy*

Studies in the Regulation of Economic Activity
TITLES PUBLISHED

Studies in the Regulation of Economic Activity

Railroads, Freight, and Public Policy

THEODORE E. KEELER

The Brookings Institution / Washington, D.C.

Library of Congress Cataloging in Publication data:

Keeler, Theodore E.
  Railroads, freight, and public policy.
  (Studies in the regulation of economic activity)
  Includes bibliographical references and index.
  1. Railroads and state—United States.
2. Railroads—United States—Freight. I. Title.
II. Series.
HE2757.K43 1983   385'.068   82-45985
ISBN 0-8157-4856-6
ISBN 0-8157-4855-8 (pbk.)

9 8 7 6 5 4 3 2 1

THE BROOKINGS INSTITUTION is an independent organization devoted to nonpartisan research, education, and publication in economics, government, foreign policy, and the social sciences generally. Its principal purposes are to aid in the development of sound public policies and to promote public understanding of issues of national importance.

The Institution was founded on December 8, 1927, to merge the activities of the Institute for Government Research, founded in 1916, the Institute of Economics, founded in 1922, and the Robert Brookings Graduate School of Economics and Government, founded in 1924.

The Board of Trustees is responsible for the general administration of the Institution, while the immediate direction of the policies, program, and staff is vested in the President, assisted by an advisory committee of the officers and staff. The by-laws of the Institution state: "It is the function of the Trustees to make possible the conduct of scientific research, and publication, under the most favorable conditions, and to safeguard the independence of the research staff in the pursuit of their studies and in the publication of the results of such studies. It is not a part of their function to determine, control, or influence the conduct of particular investigations or the conclusions reached."

The President bears final responsibility for the decision to publish a manuscript as a Brookings book. In reaching his judgment on the competence, accuracy, and objectivity of each study, the President is advised by the director of the appropriate research program and weighs the views of a panel of expert outside readers who report to him in confidence on the quality of the work. Publication of a work signifies that it is deemed a competent treatment worthy of public consideration but does not imply endorsement of conclusions or recommendations.

The Institution maintains its position of neutrality on issues of public policy in order to safeguard the intellectual freedom of the staff. Hence interpretations or conclusions in Brookings publications should be understood to be solely those of the authors and should not be attributed to the Institution, to its trustees, officers, or other staff members, or to the organizations that support its research.

Foreword

RAILROAD FREIGHT transportation has been regulated longer and more heavily than most other U.S. industries. Starting in the nineteenth century, as railroads became powerful, public policy was framed in response to monopoly tendencies and policymakers tried to ensure fair treatment of all shippers. These matters continue to be of concern, but other issues have become more urgent in recent decades. Many railroads have been abandoned or taken over by government agencies after going bankrupt, and the industry seems likely to deteriorate even further. Informed observers have concluded that government regulation has caused many of the industry's financial troubles and has led to a great waste of economic resources.

In 1969 Ann F. Friedlaender, in *The Dilemma of Freight Transport Regulation,* the first book in the Brookings Studies in the Regulation of Economic Activity series, recommended relaxation of Interstate Commerce Commission controls and substitution of cost-reducing rate competition for cost-increasing service competition among railroads. Recognizing the social costs of the existing system, Congress passed sweeping legislative reforms in 1976 and 1980 and the ICC moved rapidly to loosen government controls substantially.

This book is a thoroughgoing analysis of the economic effects of regulation before and after the 1976 and 1980 reforms. Theodore E. Keeler considers the efficiency and distributional effects of rail rate regulation, abandonment, and firm entry. He deals with taxation and subsidization policies toward railroads and competing modes of surface transport, antitrust policies toward rail mergers, and labor policies. He concludes with some recommendations intended to ensure an important and profitable role for railroads in the U.S. economy for years to come.

Theodore Keeler is professor of economics at the University of California, Berkeley. Most of the work for this book was done while he was on leave from Berkeley at Brookings, where he was a senior fellow (1980–81) and guest scholar (1981–82). He is indebted to Kenneth D.

Boyer, John F. Due, Ann F. Friedlaender, Curtis Grimm, Robert G. Harris, Richard C. Levin, Sam Peltzman, and Clifford Winston, all of whom read the manuscript and made many useful comments on it. Robert W. Crandall, Sylvester Damus, Darius Gaskins, Barry Harris, A. Scheffer Lang, Jane E. Lewin, Alexander Morton, and Robert Reynolds also provided comments that were helpful in preparing the manuscript, as did seminar groups to which some of the material in this book was presented, including those at the California Institute of Technology, the University of Chicago, Duke University, Harvard University, the University of Pennsylvania, Yale University, the U.S. Department of Justice, and the U.S. Interstate Commerce Commission. Work on the book also benefited considerably from the comments of several people in the railroad industry, including William Harris and Fred Smith of the Association of American Railroads and William Weber of Southern Pacific.

The author also gratefully acknowledges the help of those at Brookings who made the book possible. Eliot Birnbaum and Gregory Call provided diligent research assistance; Lisa Saunders typed the manuscript through several versions, with substantial help from Kirk W. Kimmell; Elizabeth H. Cross edited the manuscript; Penelope Harpold verified data and references; and Diana Regenthal prepared the index. Joseph A. Pechman provided invaluable support and encouragement along the way.

This is the twentieth publication in the Brookings series of Studies in the Regulation of Economic Activity. It was financed by grants from the Alfred P. Sloan Foundation, the Ford Foundation, the Alex C. Walker Educational and Charitable Foundation, the Andrew W. Mellon Foundation, and the Interstate Commerce Commission, as well as by sabbatical leave support from the University of California.

The views expressed here are those of the author and should not be ascribed to the foundations whose assistance is acknowledged above, to the University of California, to the Interstate Commerce Commission, or to the trustees, officers, or staff members of the Brookings Institution.

BRUCE K. MACLAURY
President

November 1982
Washington, D.C.

Contents

Contents

Figures

Railroads and Regulation

NOT ONLY is the railroad industry one of the oldest in the nation, it was also one of the first to be regulated by the government. Ever since their corporate charters gave railroads the right of eminent domain and obligated them to serve on the routes for which they received that right, public policy has closely controlled the industry.

Over the years the industry has had difficulty adjusting to changes in its market environment—to changes in tastes, in location of economic activity, and above all in competing transportation modes. These changes have resulted in familiar problems: bankrupt firms, deteriorating service on many routes, nationalization of a large amount of service, and heavy deficits, which have placed an increasing burden on taxpayers.

Many have argued that public policy toward the railroad industry has exacerbated these problems, reducing its ability to adapt to the market changes, requiring it to provide services that are no longer economic and to charge rates that are not compensatory, and in turn forcing some firms into bankruptcy. Policies alleged to have these effects include not only regulation of rates and abandonments, but also taxation and subsidization of rail and other modes, and encouragement of inefficient wages and work rules.

In response to these problems, the federal government enacted dramatic changes in rail regulatory policies in 1980, and the Reagan administration planned its budget assuming that the railroad industry would cease to be a drain on public revenues.

The aim in this book is to provide better understanding of the economic effects of public policies toward the railroad industry, past and present, and to evaluate normatively recent changes in policy. Several questions suggest themselves. What have been the goals of rail regulatory policies in the recent past? How successful have the policies been in achieving those goals? What have been their effects on economic efficiency and on the financial solvency of rail firms? From a normative economic viewpoint, are there good reasons for regulating the industry? Are the recent changes likely to increase economic efficiency? What further changes might be called for?

There is also a more general issue in positive economics to which this study can contribute—why governments regulate industries, and why they pursue the specific policies they do. For many years, it was assumed that government would undertake what public decisionmakers regarded as being in the public interest, and if it failed to do so, that was a mistake or a failure. More recently, a substantial literature has developed in economics arguing instead that government regulators deliberately follow policies quite different from their perceptions of the public interest. The theories referred to in this literature are now called "economic theories of regulation."

As possibly the oldest and still one of the most important of the regulated industries, the railroad industry is a rich source of evidence for testing certain of the economic theories of regulatory behavior. In this study those theories are extended to make them at once more general and more suitable for application to the railroad industry (and to show in more detail than heretofore how they relate to earlier public interest theories). Evidence from the industry is used to test the theories' validity.

Although positive and normative threads of the study will be pursued separately at times, they are actually intertwined, and understanding one requires understanding the other.

CHAPTER ONE

Financial Viability and Productivity of Capital

THE EXTENT to which the railroad industry is a problem for public policy depends critically on the extent of its financial problems. The public has thought of some railroads as financially weak ever since they were built. The expression "hell will freeze over when the Erie pays a dividend" dates from the nineteenth century. But this problem was not seen as being widespread, and most of the Erie's routes survived through the conversion to government ownership in 1976. Similarly, many railroads went bankrupt during the Great Depression, but most investors perceived this as merely a temporary state: when times got better, the railroads could be reorganized on a more profitable basis. Thanks to World War II and the highly profitable traffic it brought, most railroads that had been bankrupted in the 1930s were reorganized after the war.

In the 1950s, however, the problem of chronic financial difficulty arose, first for a few small carriers in depressed areas, such as the New York, Ontario, and Western, and then for stronger New England carriers, such as the New Haven and the Boston and Maine. Still, neither investors nor regulators seemed particularly concerned. Serious financial problems were still special and isolated cases; practically all other railroads were regarded as financially viable, either as they were or with modest regulatory reforms. This is substantiated by the behavior of both regulators and investors toward the merger of the New York Central and the Pennsylvania into the Penn Central in 1968. Investors bought the stock of the merged firm at what can, in retrospect, be called an extraordinarily high price. To help preserve service in New England, the regulatory authorities made acquisition of the bankrupt New Haven Railroad a condition for the merger, assuming as well that the merged firm would be profitable enough to cross-subsidize the New Haven's money-losing services. Several other northeastern railroads went bankrupt shortly before or after this, and in 1976, as the Penn Central ran out of cash, a subsidized nationalized firm, Conrail, was formed from them.

Even so, in the mid-1970s the railroad problem was regarded as mainly a northeastern phenomenon, most railroads in the rest of the country being financially sound. Nevertheless, in the late 1970s three admittedly weak railroads in the West went bankrupt, the Katy, the Rock Island, and the Milwaukee. Rumors of the imminent bankruptcy of another railroad in the Midwest and South, the Illinois Central Gulf, have been sufficiently persistent to move its president to issue several strong statements that his railroad is not going bankrupt.[1]

It is obviously worth knowing the extent to which this financial problem in the railroad industry is a regional one, and the likelihood of its spreading to other parts of the system. Similarly, the evaluation of any program of regulatory reform for the industry should take some account of the impact of that program on rail profitability. For these reasons, a detailed analysis of the financial viability of the industry is appropriate. The emphasis here will be on evidence before 1980, for two reasons. First, as this was written, detailed evidence for subsequent years was not yet available. Second, analysis of pre-1980 data enables analysis of the industry before the regulatory reforms of 1980 were implemented. Any post-1979 financial results that are available will be analyzed in chapter 5.

Financial Viability

Economic criteria for financial viability are fairly precise in theory but, like many numbers in economics, hard to measure empirically. Theoretically, a firm (or component of a firm) is financially viable if its capital is earning an opportunity cost, or what an investment of equivalent risk could earn on the average elsewhere in the economy. If, in addition, some of the firm's investments are "sunk" and never need be made again to keep the firm running (for instance, certain grading of the land on which railroad tracks run), then the firm need only earn scrap or liquidation value on that investment. It is not a priori clear what investments should be regarded as sunk; that depends on how long the

1. Frank Malone, "ICG: Slimming Down and Shaping Up," *Railway Age,* vol. 180 (November 26, 1979), pp. 34–35.

firm continues to operate. Thus if a locomotive with an expected remaining life of ten years is to be treated as a sunk cost, the firm should plan to go out of business (or eliminate the business using the locomotive) in ten years. In calculating its total opportunity cost of capital, the firm should value capital items not treated as sunk at their replacement cost—what it would cost to replace them at current prices and technology.

Calculating these returns to capital from a firm's cost and revenue accounts and balance sheets is difficult and at best imprecise, and many would argue that the best evidence on the financial viability of an industry can be gleaned from financial markets. That indicates how much investors have earned in the firm in income and capital gains, and can be compared with returns on investment for other securities of equivalent risk. There are two difficulties with using evidence from securities markets for railroads. First, a very large number of railroads are held by diversified holding companies involved in many types of industries. Often these industries are related to the railroads in the sense that they exploit minerals and timber resources available on railroad land. Second, nonrail uses of rail properties can be factored into the values of rail securities whether the railroad is diversified or not. Indeed, as investors in Penn Central found out, high values for rail securities can even be justified by the potential for government buy-out of a money-losing private railroad for public operation. In this study, therefore, although limited use is made of security values in determining the viability of the industry, considerable use must be made of accounting data.

Historical Accounting Data

As a first-round approximation for estimates of rail financial viability, some detailed historical evidence based on relatively conventional accounting data for two dozen major railroads in the United States is presented. The question is, how has the railroad industry fared in profitability relative to the corporate sector as a whole since World War II? The analysis here is based on book (historical) values of capital, with a correction for different treatments of taxes and depreciation between the rail and nonrail sectors.

Such a long-term historical comparison is likely to be revealing for several reasons. First, because the average lifetime of rail capital is considerably longer than that of capital in the rest of the corporate sector, the use of book values tends to overstate the rail return relative to that in other sectors, since rail capital is older and, because of inflation, valued lower. Railroads that fail to earn an opportunity cost based on this comparison are unlikely to be earning an opportunity cost based on any other comparison.

Second, it is often argued that while most railroads do poorly in their return on historical values of investment, they would do much better if their capital asset bases were written off to eliminate sunk costs. This might be true at any one time, but if a firm fails to earn its opportunity cost of capital based on historical values over a long time, say, thirty-five years, it is unlikely to be viable: most fixed costs should be variable, even on railroads, over such a long period.

Third, direct comparison of returns on investment in railroads with returns in the corporate sector as a whole assumes that the risk levels are equivalent. Evidence on risk levels indicates that, although they do vary considerably from railroad to railroad just as they do throughout the corporate sector, except for railroads nearing bankruptcy, the *overall* level of risk for rail investors on the average does not differ greatly from that for other corporate investors.[2] Although direct comparison of rates of return might generate unreasonable comparisons for some roads, it should be a generally reasonable procedure. The evidence also indicates that it is the poorer railroads, the ones closer to bankruptcy, for which the risks are higher. Thus, if anything, comparing rates of return should bias the analysis against the rich railroads and in the direction of the poorer ones (the poorer ones will appear to be more viable than they are).

Returns in the Corporate Sector

Before the returns for railroads are considered, it is necessary to analyze the return for the corporate sector as a whole, which can serve

2. The most widely accepted measure of the risk level confronted by investors in a firm is the "beta coefficient" for that firm. It measures the amount of risk inherent in a firm's securities that cannot be eliminated by diversifying a portfolio. See, for example, Michael C. Jensen, "Capital Markets: Theory and Evidence," *Bell Journal of Economics,* vol. 3 (Autumn 1972), pp. 357–98. A beta coefficient of one implies a risk level equal to the average for all corporations in the securities market, with a lower beta corresponding to a lower risk. Here are some recent betas for some major railroads: Chicago and Northwestern, 1.50; CSX, 0.90; Florida East Coast, 0.80; Kansas City Southern, 1.10; Norfolk and Western, 0.85; Rio Grande, 1.30; Soo Line, 0.75; Southern, 0.90. These betas come from *Value Line,* April 10, 1981, pp. 306–14.

Table 1-1. Returns on Investment of All U.S. Nonfinancial Corporations, 1946–79

Percent

Description	1946–50	1951–55	1956–60	1961–65	1966–70	1971–75	1976–79
1. Gross return (book value), including state, local, and federal taxes	15.4	15.3	14.0	15.1[a]	15.5	16.8	19.4[b]
2. Net return (replacement value)							
a. Not including state and local taxes	12.2	11.3	9.4	11.2	11.0	8.3	8.5
b. Including state and local taxes	13.2	12.3	10.5	12.5	12.4	9.6	9.5
3. Gross return (replacement value)							
a. Not including state and local taxes	11.6	11.4	10.6	12.0	11.7	9.5	n.a.
b. Including state[a] and local taxes	12.6	12.4	11.7	13.3	13.1	10.8	n.a.

Sources: Line 1 calculated by author from Internal Revenue Service, *Statistics of Income: Corporation Income Tax Returns*, 1946–75; lines 2a and 2b from Martin Feldstein and James Poterba, "State and Local Taxes and the Rate of Return on Nonfinancial Corporate Capital," Harvard Institute of Economic Research, Discussion Paper 800 (November 1980), p. 10; line 3a from Martin Feldstein and Lawrence Summers, "Is the Rate of Profit Falling?" *Brookings Papers on Economic Activity, 1:1977*, p. 216; line 3b calculated by author from the above figures by the following formula: line 3a plus line 2b minus line 2a.

n.a. Not available.

a. 1962 data excluded because of insufficient information.

b. 1976–78 only.

as a benchmark for the railroad analysis. As might be expected, measuring something so broad as the return in the corporate sector of the U.S. economy cannot be done with precision, and there are several different series from which to choose, as shown in table 1-1.

Most directly comparable with the historical series is that calculated in line 1 of the table. This is based on historical values with a gross return on gross value of capital (consistent with the assumption of constant productivity of capital goods over their lifetimes), and it includes in the return all taxes, state, local, and federal. (It is desirable to include taxes in the return, because then it measures the full social profitability of investments in an industry, correcting for differences in tax treatment of industries, which might artificially distort returns.)

The other results presented in the table, all based on replacement values of capital, come from the work of Feldstein and others. The series most comparable with my calculations is that of gross return on gross capital stock, with state and local taxes included in the return (line 3b). Since they did not explicitly calculate this combination, an estimate was made from two of their series.[3]

3. See source note for calculating line 3b in table 1-1.

Comparison of the results of table 1-1 shows that the return on investment achieved in the corporate sector is somewhat sensitive to the assumptions used for the calculations. But the differences in the results are quite consistent with a priori expectations: because of inflation, the investment base calculated by replacement value is higher than when calculated by book value. So the return based on replacement value is consistently lower than the return based on book value. In any event, no matter what method is used, the evidence in table 1-1 probably makes it safe to conclude that no railroad is earning its opportunity cost of capital unless it is earning over 15 percent, based on book value, or over 10 percent, based on replacement value. Indeed, no series that includes state and local taxes registers a return lower than 14 percent on book value or 10.8 percent on replacement value at any time since 1960. Although the post-1975 evidence is skimpy, what there is certainly suggests a return at least that high for the most recent period, 1976–79. And a strong argument could be made for a considerably higher return on investment—12 percent on replacement value—based on Feldstein's series of gross return on gross assets, corrected for the inclusion of state and local taxes.

Returns for Railroads

Based on calculations similar to those done for all corporations, evidence for railroads is presented in tables 1-2 and 1-3. Table 1-2 contains long-term series, from 1946 through 1979, for a sample of twenty-four railroads, most of them the major firms, and shorter series for six others. Table 1-3 presents returns for the remaining Class I railroads for 1976–79. (Details of the calculations for these returns and data sources are given in appendix A.) As in previous studies of railroad costs, data are averaged over five-year periods to reflect the fact that railroad accounts treat some capital investments as current accounts. The purchase of rails and ties, for example, is treated as a current expense rather than a capital one. In good years railroads invest heavily in rails and ties, and profits are understated; in bad years, they defer maintenance, and profits are overstated. (Ideally, rails and ties should be depreciated, and for a more limited sample I shall do so.) The results shown in tables 1-2 and 1-3 are especially striking in one way: in the twenty years from 1959 to 1979 relatively few railroads earned a return as high as the corporate sector as a whole did. A number of railroads

Table 1-2. Returns on Investment of Major Railroads, 1946–79

Percent

Railroad	1946–50	1951–55	1956–60	1961–65	1966–70	1971–75	1976–79
Atchison, Topeka & Santa Fe	8.8	9.6	7.7	6.7	6.1	6.8	7.1
Baltimore & Ohio	6.6	7.3	5.6	4.4	5.5	7.0	8.2
Burlington Northern (Great Northern)	7.0	7.9	6.7	6.0	5.1	4.6	5.1
Chesapeake & Ohio	9.2	10.5	9.7	7.3	6.6	7.1	4.7
Chicago, Burlington & Quincy	8.9	8.2	5.7	5.3	4.8[a]	. . .	. . .
Chicago, Milwaukee, St. Paul & Pacific	4.3	4.3	3.9	4.3	3.4	2.3	−4.9
Chicago & Northwestern	3.6	3.3	2.9	4.1	3.0	7.0	6.7
Chicago, Rock Island & Pacific	7.0	7.0	4.9	4.0	1.6	−2.0	−2.0[a]
Cincinnati, New Orleans & Texas Pacific	14.3	17.8	12.0	6.8	9.2	12.8	17.6
Conrail New York Central	4.4	5.9	5.2	4.4	4.3[a]	. . .	. . .
Pennsylvania	4.0	5.9	4.8	4.7	1.8	−1.3	−22.7
Denver & Rio Grande Western	6.4	10.8	10.8	9.7	9.8	10.2	10.8
Florida East Coast	3.2	4.3	4.0	4.0	3.7	9.6	8.6
Gulf, Mobile & Ohio	7.1	8.9	5.4	5.2	6.3	4.5[a]	. . .
Illinois Central Gulf	10.8	9.7	6.4	5.3	5.2	5.0[a]	2.5
Louisville & Nashville	7.5	9.5	6.8	6.1	6.2	6.7	6.2
Missouri Pacific	5.9	6.0	6.4	6.4	5.9	6.8	9.4
New York, New Haven & Hartford	3.8	4.2	1.7	−0.9	−1.6[a]	. . .	. . .
Norfolk & Western	9.9	10.6	10.6	11.1	8.8	9.0	10.8
Northern Pacific	5.4	5.0	4.5	3.8	3.9[a]	. . .	. . .
Pittsburgh & Lake Erie	12.2	13.0	9.4	10.3	9.6	7.7	11.3
Richmond, Fredericksburg & Potomac	10.3	13.0	11.9	10.4	12.2	13.6	13.2[a]
St. Louis–San Francisco	5.9	7.5	5.5	5.9	6.9	6.3	7.4
Seaboard Coast Line (Seaboard)	6.6	9.5	7.5	6.7	5.7	5.9	7.8
Seaboard Coast Line (Atlantic Coast Line)	4.0	5.5	4.6	5.8	6.2[a]	. . .	. . .
Soo Line	3.8	4.0	3.8	4.8	5.7	8.4	10.7
Southern	7.4	10.8	9.8	9.1	9.3	9.0	9.2
Southern Pacific	7.8	7.9	5.6	6.4	6.8	6.9	5.8
Union Pacific	7.6	8.1	7.8	7.8	8.0	9.6	10.8
Western Pacific	6.3	8.5	6.1	6.6	3.9	4.7	6.7

Sources: See appendix A.

a. Average for portion of period during which the railroad operated.

generally thought to be relatively prosperous have earned less than an opportunity cost of capital since World War II. Admittedly, staying in business may not generally require earning the full average return on investment in the corporate sector. According to the criterion of earning somewhere near the average return for the corporate sector, a significant

Table 1-3. Returns on Investment of Other Class I Railroads, 1976–79

Percent

Railroad	Return
Alabama Great Southern	8.9
Bessemer & Lake Erie	14.7
Boston & Maine	0.4
Central of Georgia	10.9
Clinchfield	21.2
Colorado & Southern	2.6
Delaware & Hudson	−4.9
Detroit, Toledo & Ironton	5.1
Duluth, Missabe & Iron Range	6.8
Elgin, Joliet & Eastern	17.6
Grand Trunk Western	3.9
Kansas City Southern	8.9
Missouri-Kansas-Texas	2.1
St. Louis–Southwestern	10.5
Western Maryland	8.7

Sources: Same as table 1-2.

number of railroads have indeed earned an opportunity cost of capital over the past few years. These include the Rio Grande, the Norfolk and Western, the Pittsburgh and Lake Erie, the Richmond, Fredericksburg, and Potomac, the Soo Line, the Southern (and its highly profitable subsidiary, the Cincinnati, New Orleans, and Texas Pacific), and the Union Pacific. Based on book value accounting, these firms all earned returns on investment above, equal to, or slightly below those earned by the corporate sector as a whole, and for the most part did so fairly consistently. These railroads thus appear to be financially viable. Very near this group, though not quite so steadily so, are the Florida East Coast and the Missouri Pacific. Below this is another group of less profitable firms, but ones still regarded as prosperous by many, that earn no better than a 6 to 7 percent return on investment, relative to an opportunity cost of 10 percent. These include the Santa Fe, the Baltimore and Ohio, the Chicago and Northwestern (whose return on investment is biased upward because nearly $300 million worth of its assets were written off in a transfer of ownership in 1972), the Louisville and Nashville, the Frisco (now merged with the Burlington Northern), the Seaboard Coast Line, and the Western Pacific. Their reputations for having newer equipment and well-manicured plants give most of these companies an image of affluence, yet they fail to earn an opportunity cost of capital. Unless the accounting procedures used here are considerably understating their returns relative to those of the corporate sector, it is reasonable to ask whether future private investments in the rail components of their businesses will be justified. It might rightly be argued, however, that these return-on-investment numbers contain a disproportionate amount of sunk costs, and that if one wrote them off and calculated incremental returns to new investments, the return would be higher. This is done for a number of railroads in this group later.

Another group, while not insolvent, nevertheless is earning a return on investment well below half that in the corporate sector. This group includes the Burlington Northern, the Chesapeake and Ohio, the Illinois Central Gulf, and the Southern Pacific. With returns on investment of only about 2½ to 5 percent, these firms must have higher returns soon if their rail operations are to be viable on a long-term basis. There is not nearly enough evidence on any one of these railroads to predict bankruptcy, and investors in them have the benefits of diversified operations in most cases. But firms such as the Rock Island, the New York Central, and the Pennsylvania were earning returns of 2 to 5 percent.

The final group of firms in the sample had negative returns on investment for the 1975–79 period or earlier, and they are all either bankrupt or government-owned (the large losses shown for Conrail presumably reflect heavy spending of public funds to revitalize a run-down plant in the late 1970s).

Calculations were made for the remaining Class I railroads for 1975–79 and the results are shown in table 1-3. Of these, some, such as the Bessemer and Lake Erie, the Clinchfield, and the Cotton Belt (St. Louis–Southwestern, a subsidiary of the Southern Pacific), apparently earn sufficient returns to make them somewhere near financially viable. Others, such as the Boston and Maine and the Missouri-Kansas-Texas, both in states of bankruptcy, clearly do not earn adequate returns.

If these results are correct, a large fraction of the nation's rail service is currently being provided at an economic loss. Before assessing the significance of the results, it is appropriate to check them against some alternative calculations based on more realistic valuations of the rate base.

Economic Valuation of the Rail Rate Base

The use of book values to calculate railroad returns on investment introduces two previously mentioned biases that work in opposite directions. First, it includes sunk costs, so that the incremental return to new investments is likely to be higher. Second, it fails to take into account the inflation of recent years, thus understating the rate base and overstating the rate of return. (If rail capital is longer-lived than all corporate capital, this applies to rail relative to the rest of the economy.) It is therefore best to calculate returns on investment that write off sunk costs but increase those not sunk to account for inflation. This measure should be compared with a similarly corrected rate-of-return series for the corporate sector as a whole.

The third bias in the calculations is their treatment of rail and tie investments as current maintenance expenditures. A more accurate measure of the return on investment can be achieved by depreciating them and including them in the rate base, as for other capital investments.

The following calculations correct for these biases, though for a limited sample of times and firms. The size of the sample was restricted by such things as data availability, accounting changes (sometimes caused by mergers), and the sheer cost of the data collection and computation involved in doing these corrected calculations.

For two reasons, firms that are bankrupt are clearly not the best for inclusion in the sample. First, one hardly needs to go through these calculations to determine that such firms are not viable. Second, firms that have deferred their maintenance over a long period of time are unlikely to give accurate estimates of their viability anyway, because making the road viable will entail many hidden rehabilitation costs not evident in their accounts.[4] I therefore restrict my sample to railroads classified as viable and near-viable in the above analysis, that is, ones that earn a return on investment of over 5 percent and that have a reputation for having maintained their plant and equipment well over the past few years. If these more accurate calculations show that firms in this group fare about the same as the corporate sector, one can be reasonably sure that the remaining firms in the sample would do no better than they did in the previous comparison if they too were compared on a more accurate basis. I therefore selected five carriers for these revised calculations: the Santa Fe, the Chesapeake and Ohio, the Rio Grande, the Southern, and the Union Pacific.

The calculations are described in detail in appendix A. For purposes of comparison with the rest of the corporate economy, I used the

4. For estimates of these costs, see, for example, Brock Adams, *A Prospectus for Change in the Railroad Freight Industry* (U.S. Department of Transportation, 1979).

Table 1-4. Rates of Return for Selected Railroads, Based on Replacement Valuation of Rate Base with Sunk Costs Written Off

	Railroad[a]					Corporate sector	
						Gross	Net
Description	ATSF	C&O	D&RGW	SOU	UP	value	value
Book value[b]							
1971–75	6.7	7.2	10.3	9.0	9.6	9.9	n.a.
1976–79	6.3	4.3	10.1	8.1	9.4	n.a.	n.a.
Replacement value, standard treatment of rails and ties							
1971–75	5.8	5.8	8.8	7.8	7.7	10.8	9.6
1976–79	3.8	2.5	6.8	5.1	5.9	n.a.	9.5
Replacement value, depreciation of rails and ties							
1971–75	6.2	6.1	9.2	8.7	8.0	10.8	9.6
1976–79	4.3	2.9	7.7	6.2[c]	6.5[d]	n.a.	9.5

Sources: See appendix A.
n.a. Not availble.
a.   ATSF = Atchison, Topeka & Santa Fe
     C&O = Chesapeake & Ohio
   D&RGW = Denver & Rio Grande Western
     SOU = Southern
      UP = Union Pacific.
b. From tables 1-1 to 1-3.
c. 1976–77 only.
d. 1976–78 only.

estimates of the return on replacement value for the nonfinancial corporate sector done by Feldstein and his associates at Harvard University. Overall, the railroad figures, as calculated, overstate the rail return relative to that in the corporate sector as a whole because all investments made more than twenty-five years before the year in question are written off as sunk costs: values of right-of-way, grading, and older tracks and roadbeds are ignored. The calculations of Feldstein and others for the corporate sector, on the other hand, made no such write-offs of sunk costs.

The results of these comparisons are shown in table 1-4. They indicate that, if anything, the earlier calculations based on book values overstate rail profitability. In each case the rail return on investment calculated by this more accurate method is lower than that calculated by the earlier method, and in some cases, dramatically so. No railroad passes the test of a 10 percent return on investment. Still, the Rio Grande, the Southern, and the Union Pacific come reasonably close. On the other hand, the

Santa Fe and the Chesapeake and Ohio, as before, continue to earn a return on investment distinctly below normal.

These calculations also make it evident that, for railroads that keep their plant and equipment in good condition, inclusion of rail and tie expenses in the capital account rather than the current one has little effect on the results. To the extent that a railroad fails to keep up its plant and equipment, of course, the conventional treatment of rail and tie expenses (in the current as opposed to capital account) will tend to understate the current return on investment if that return is to measure the firm's long-term viability.

The evidence from this admittedly small sample of calculations thus shows that the change to this more accurate accounting method has practically no effect on the results; it merely indicates that calculations based on book values will in all likelihood overstate rail profitability.

Financial Markets

Although interpreting evidence from financial markets for railroads is subject to pitfalls, it should be useful in corroborating the accounting results. Specifically, if a railroad is earning its cost of capital, the market should capitalize the value of its assets at or above the replacement value (with sunk costs valued at scrap, as before). As noted, for a railroad to earn such an economic return on its replacement value, it must do so on its book value as well. Therefore, a measure of a railroad's viability can be derived by comparing the capitalized stock market value of its shares with its book value. If the market capitalizes the value of its shares below book value, the firm's assets, whether in rail or nonrail uses, are capable of earning an opportunity cost of capital. For these calculations, it is of course necessary to select firms involved more or less exclusively in the railroad industry and exclude firms with much business in real estate and natural resources.

Results of these calculations for 1981 are shown in table 1-5. In interpreting these results, it is well to recall that at that time the railroad industry was enjoying the greatest stock market boom in many years.

If anything, the previous calculations are confirmed. The Norfolk and Western, Rio Grande, Soo, and Southern are all capitalized just below book value, implying that if they fall short of earning an opportunity cost, it is not by much. And two small southern firms, the Kansas City

Table 1-5. Financial Market Valuation of Rail Assets, Spring 1981

Railroad	Recent price per share (dollars)	Book value per share, 1980 (dollars)	Valuation ratio
Chicago & Northwestern	66.00	26.21	2.52
CSX Corporation[a]	54.00	70.32	.77
Florida East Coast	93.00	71.89	1.29
Kansas City Southern	48.00	39.65[b]	1.21
Norfolk & Western	47.00	48.10	.98
Denver & Rio Grande Western	44.00	48.81	.90
Soo Line	27.00	27.89	.97
Southern	89.00	83.50	.94

Source: *Value Line*, April 10, 1981, pp. 306–14.
a. Includes the Chesapeake & Ohio, Baltimore & Ohio, Western Maryland, Seaboard Coast Line, Louisville & Nashville, and Clinchfield.
b. *Value Line* estimate.

Southern and the Florida East Coast, are capitalized above book value. (The results for the Chicago and Northwestern are suspect because of the previously mentioned 1972 write-off of its assets.) On the other hand, the Southern Pacific and the CSX Corporation (including the Chesapeake and Ohio, Baltimore and Ohio, Western Maryland, Seaboard Coast Line, Louisville and Nashville, and Clinchfield) are capitalized well below book value, consistent with the result that none of these roads except the Clinchfield are earning an opportunity cost of capital.

Although in general similar inferences cannot be drawn for railroads involved in considerable nonrail business, one piece of evidence on the Burlington Northern is relevant. To quote *Forbes* magazine: "Buy a share of BN at today's $71 market price, and, in effect, you are buying the underlying resources and getting the railroad for free."[5] This may make the railroad a bargain, as *Forbes* states, or it may simply imply that the financial markets attach low value to the Burlington Northern Railroad's earning power. The results shown in table 1-2 on the Burlington Northern's return on investment make the latter interpretation appear reasonable.

This suggests that the preceding analysis of rail profits is consistent with the financial markets of the railroad industry. It follows that if the industry does not earn a higher rate of return in the near future, pressure for shrinkage of the system will continue.

5. Paul Gibson, "A Railroad for the Long Haul," *Forbes* (April 27, 1981), p. 126.

The Financial Problem

The results presented in the preceding sections suggested that a considerable number of railroad firms fall far short of earning an opportunity cost of capital and will have to improve their return, receive public subsidies, or go out of the railroad business in the not-too-distant future. But the extensiveness of the problem cannot be measured by the number of firms facing difficulties. A more appropriate measure would be either the amount of freight carried by troubled firms or the fraction of the route system accounted for. And there is no clear-cut line between financial health and bankruptcy.

To analyze the extent of the railroad problem, railroad firms are first divided into the rough classifications of financial viability shown in table 1-6. The top category, with a 9 percent return on investment or better, still does not necessarily correspond to earning a full opportunity cost of capital (15 percent or so on book value), and only a tiny fraction of the railroads do this well.

Indeed, it is not clear that any firms meet the theoretically appropriate criterion of earning an opportunity cost of capital on the replacement value of their asset bases (with sunk costs written off). Certainly none of the major and relatively prosperous firms listed in table 1-4 can pass this test, although it is possible that some of the smaller ones—such as the Southern's subsidiary, the Cincinnati, New Orleans, and Texas Pacific—might do so. Thus a regulatory agency trying to set rail rate ceilings would have great difficulty in denying railroads rate increases because their returns on investment were too high.

Table 1-6. Financial Problems of Railroads
Percent

Classification	Return on book investment before taxes	Portion of system accounted for	
		Freight revenues	Route-miles
A. Viable or nearly so	Over 9	30.1	26.5
B. Marginally viable	7–9	22.5	24.0
C. Unlikely to be viable	4–7	26.2	25.7
D. Financial problems likely	0–4	21.2	23.7

Source: Derived from preceding tables.

Despite the evidence that practically no railroad earns a full opportunity cost of capital, firms earning over 9 percent on book value are classified as likely to be financially viable for several reasons. First, relatively minor structural changes, such as rate changes, are most likely to make these firms viable. Second, by definition only a fraction of firms in the economy (say, half) earn an average rate of return or better. In the general scheme of things, some firms will end up earning below the average return for the corporate sector (though presumably not far below) and still survive. Admittedly, any decision on what return is needed to maintain viability is somewhat arbitrary, but in defense of the selection of the 9 percent boundary, it is worth noting that the Southern, which earns slightly over 9 percent on book value (though its subsidiaries are more profitable), seems to have relatively little difficulty financing new investments and also seems to achieve favorable valuation of its assets by the capital markets.

Firms earning a 7 to 9 percent return are classified as marginally viable because, though they are clearly not earning an opportunity cost of capital, they may be close to doing so without too drastic a change in their rates, routes served, and so on.

On the other hand, firms earning less than a 7 percent return (remember, this return does not have any income or property taxes netted out) fall far short of viability, and there is good reason to doubt that a firm in this category would earn an adequate rate of return without drastic changes, whether these entailed mergers, service abandonments, rate changes, labor practices, or other major structural shifts. Firms in this group are thus classified as not viable with existing structure and regulations.

Firms earning returns of under 4 percent would have to be classified as having serious financial problems, and firms earning under 2 percent (including negative returns) are more often than not in a state of bankruptcy or (in the case of Conrail) subsidized government ownership.

The classification scheme presented in table 1-6 probably overstates the fraction of the nation's rail system operated by viable firms. Even so, it is striking how small a fraction of the system could be called viable: firms classified as "viable or nearly so" account for only 30.1 percent of the nation's freight revenues and 26.5 percent of the route-mileage. Firms classified as "unlikely to be viable" or worse account for nearly half the freight revenues and over half the route-mileage in the system. And the rail financial problem extends geographically throughout the nation: firms classified below "marginally viable" include not only Conrail in the Northeast, but also the Illinois Central in the Midwest and South, and the Burlington Northern and the Southern Pacific, both of which have vast and important route networks in the West.

These results are subject to some further qualifications, for they can be easily misinterpreted. They do not imply, for example, that firms classified as less than viable are bad buys on the stock market, for the market has probably already capitalized downward the value of the railroad, and the management may well be disinvesting in the railroad in a way to optimize the firm's profitability.

Nor do these results imply that routes operated by firms classified as less than viable should or will be abandoned. Just as firms classified as viable have some routes and services they would probably like to eliminate, so firms classified as less than viable have some routes that are likely to be viable on a commercial basis. And probably changes in such areas as rate flexibility, work rules, and possibly mergers could make nonviable firms viable without any service abandonments at all.

Despite these qualifications, the results presented here do have some strong implications. The most important is that, without some dramatic structural changes in regulations, work rules, or services provided, a very large fraction of the nation's rail freight service (half or more) would be too unprofitable to be provided by private firms.

CHAPTER TWO

A Capsule History
of Railroad Regulation

A HISTORY of rail freight regulation in the United States, describing how regulation came about, why it exists, and what the laws have come to mean, is necessary for the subsequent analysis of public policies and the economic causes and effects of railroad freight regulation.

The Beginning

Most studies of rail freight regulation mark its onset (and the onset of just about all freight regulation) with the Interstate Commerce Act of 1887, or possibly with the numerous state regulatory laws passed in the 1870s and 1880s. While this is to some degree true, much of the important regulation affecting railroads today goes back far beyond that and is far more ingrained in the legal system.

Railroads are common carriers, and the important laws affecting common carriage originated in medieval British common law.[1] At that time, stagecoach, and later canal and turnpike, operators were given operating franchises, called certificates of public convenience and necessity. These franchises, issued by the government, initially reflected widespread economic cartelization practiced through the system of medieval guilds. But the notion of common carriage, and of certificates

---

1. This discussion of the common law origins of common carriage regulation draws on Stuart Daggett, *Principles of Inland Transportation* (Harper, 1928), chaps. 26–29; and Dudley F. Pegrum, "Restructuring the Transport System," in Ernest W. Williams, Jr., ed., *The Future of American Transportation* (Prentice-Hall, 1971), pp. 59–82, especially pp. 63–68. Another good reference is Sallyanne Peyton, "The Duty to Serve in the Presence of New Competition," in Werner Sichel and Thomas G. Gies, eds., *Applications of Economic Principles in Public Utility Industries* (University of Michigan Press, 1981), pp. 121–52.

granting firms franchises for common carriage, survived even as guilds disappeared.

There are several reasons for continued government controls of transportation through the sixteenth, seventeenth, and eighteenth centuries in England and then in the United States. First, stagecoaches often traveled through dangerous areas, and the government felt that, in return for franchise protection and the profits that afforded, transportation companies should be ready to bear the risks involved and assume liability for losses of and damages to passengers. Second, it was thought that regularly scheduled, reliable transportation to various regions was so important that it needed the protection of legal sanction beyond what the marketplace might supply. This meant, for example, that the carrier would be legally obligated to accept all traffic for which it had room and which was willing to pay the going rates. Third, with the advent of canals, turnpikes, and railroads, the carrier required powers over others not usually needed by commercial firms in order to function: to acquire a right-of-way, it was necessary to have powers of eminent domain so that, with reasonable compensation, the carrier could force owners of land along its right-of-way to surrender the land.

In short, the notion behind common carriage was that the government would grant the carrier certain powers and privileges, generally conferring an exclusive right to make a profit from transportation. In return for these privileges, the carrier was expected to assume certain obligations.

Long before any regulatory agency controlled entry and rates in transportation, therefore, transportation companies were bound, both by common law and by explicit corporate charters, to do many of the things now attributed to regulation by commissions. Railroads and common carriers were expected to fulfill the following conditions, both in England and in the United States:

1. The carrier may not refuse to serve.
2. The carrier must serve at a reasonable price.
3. The carrier must serve all equally.
4. The carrier is responsible for the safe delivery of the goods or persons committed to its care.[2]

Such conditions might seem too general to be viewed as regulation. But many of the regulatory constraints today believed to be onerous for railroads arose under common law as interpreted by courts. For example, the condition that rates be reasonable was used to block the use of bulk

2. Daggett, *Principles of Inland Transportation*, p. 285.

rail contract rates in interstate movement well before there was an Interstate Commerce Commission.[3] Similarly, the duty to provide service was interpreted to mean that a carrier could not freely discontinue service once it had started it: under common law and corporate charters, the courts blocked efforts to discontinue service without a full hearing involving all parties objecting.[4]

To this day, the state corporate charters that enabled railroads, and before them canal and turnpike companies, to start service long ago represent a severe regulatory constraint. The charters not only controlled the matters controlled by other corporate charters, such as amount of stock issued and size of the board of directors, but also granted eminent domain and stated specifically the routes on which the railroad would be required to provide service within the state. Unless overruled by the Interstate Commerce Commission, these charters are still legally binding on the railroads.

Another aspect of public policy toward railroads, consistent with the notion that firms were granted considerable privileges for which they in turn had responsibilities, was that of subsidization. American railroads received much aid in the form of land grants, and such grants, worth considerable sums of money, were made throughout the country. Land grants in the West are the best known of these.[5]

As the railroad industry grew in the nineteenth century, regulation by corporate charter and common law became more and more difficult. Different courts could easily disagree on what constituted reasonable rates, and the charters themselves sometimes imposed conflicting regulations on railroads (a few states attempted to set rates in the charters, for example). And as nineteenth century rail transportation and the amounts of commodities carried grew, the volume and complexity of rate problems pointed to the need for regulatory agencies more specialized than general courts of law.

Furthermore, the pricing behavior of the railroads during the middle and late nineteenth century made consistent control of rail rates politically more and more imperative. Rate wars periodically broke out on

3. *Hays* v. *Pennsylvania*, 12 Fed. 309–15, 1882. See Daggett, *Principles of Inland Transportation*, pp. 315–16.

4. Daggett, *Principles of Inland Transportation*, pp. 306–07.

5. England granted new railroads special tax advantages. Cities and states throughout the United States gave railroads substantial amounts of subsidies in the form of both money and land. See ibid., pp. 66–67.

routes served by rivals, and rates fell to levels generally believed to be unprofitable on those routes.[6] On monopoly routes rates tended to stay extremely high by comparison. The railroads disliked the rate wars and attempted to form cartels (pools) and collude on rates and services to prevent them. But the cartels generally failed shortly after they were formed, with one or more firms breaking pricing agreements. Shippers on monopoly routes also disliked the structure of rates because they found themselves paying rates far higher than those charged on competitive routes for equivalent services. Small shippers objected when large shippers received lower rates, whether the rates were based on lower costs or on market power. Because of the number of shipments and inconsistencies among the courts, the courts basing decisions on common law were unwilling or unable to solve these problems to the satisfaction of those involved, so in the 1870s state regulatory agencies were set up.[7] But states often attempted to impose contradictory terms on railroads providing interstate service, and in 1886 the Supreme Court ruled that the states were not empowered to regulate interstate commerce.[8]

The Interstate Commerce Act of 1887

All these occurrences made it evident by the mid-1880s that federal regulation of railroad rates and services would be necessary and that a federal agency would have to be established for this purpose. After a period of deliberation, Congress passed the Interstate Commerce Act of 1887.[9]

Like the British Canals and Railways Act of 1854, after which it was patterned, the Interstate Commerce Act of 1887 attempted to make explicit and achieve consistent enforcement of a number of legal principles already embedded in common law. The 1887 act required that rates

6. Gabriel Kolko, *Railroads and Regulation, 1877–1916* (Princeton University Press, 1965); and Paul MacAvoy, *The Economic Effects of Regulation: The Trunk-Line Railroad Cartels and the Interstate Commerce Commission before 1900* (MIT Press, 1965).

7. For a discussion of early state regulation of railroads, see George H. Miller, *Railroads and the Granger Laws* (University of Wisconsin Press, 1971).

8. *Wabash, St. Louis, and Pacific* v. *Illinois,* 118 U.S. 557, 1886.

9. Although this act is often regarded as the beginning of railroad regulation in this country, the discussion above should make it evident that it was not—rather, it was an evolutionary change in regulations that have persisted over the life of the industry.

be just and reasonable, prohibited discrimination against persons or shippers and undue preferences among areas, and forbade the practice of charging more for a short haul than a longer one. In practically each case, court decisions based on common law were going the same way. But most important, the act not only made these laws explicit, but also, to achieve yet more consistency, established the Interstate Commerce Commission to rule upon the law. The act also went beyond the common law substantively in some ways. It forbade the practice of pooling—that is, of colluding to control the amount of service provided and pooling equipment in that service—to ensure that no one "cheated" and expanded service beyond the agreed-upon levels.

By itself, the 1887 act was not, however, sufficient to achieve the consistency of laws and enforcement that Congress had sought—courts soon found loopholes, which subsequent amendments filled in. The Elkins Act of 1903 stated the punishments for discriminatory pricing; the Hepburn Act of 1906 gave the ICC the right to set maximum rates; and the Mann-Elkins Act of 1910 plugged a loophole in the provision prohibiting higher rates for short hauls than for longer ones.

By 1910, then, the Interstate Commerce Commission had in actuality all the powers the 1887 act intended it to have. And it used these powers in a politically effective way, for most of those who had wanted rail regulation seemed to get what they wanted. Farmers and others on low-density monopoly routes no longer felt they were objects of discrimination. The "right" of small shippers to pay rates no higher than large shippers was enforced relatively consistently and was no longer dependent on the ability of the courts to give consistent interpretation to the common law.

On the other hand, the railroads had reason to be pleased with the results as well: the officially sanctioned maximum rates that the ICC imposed on various routes served as a better stabilizer of profitable rates than any previous pools had done. Rate wars were averted, rail profitability improved, and risk to rail investors was significantly reduced.[10] In short, although various shippers unquestionably benefited from ICC rate regulation, from the firms' viewpoint ICC regulation had about it the quality of a government cartel.[11]

This cartelization was evident not only in railroad profits, but also in

10. Sam Peltzman, "Toward a More General Theory of Regulation," *Journal of Law and Economics,* vol. 19 (August 1976), pp. 211–44, especially p. 230.

11. Kolko, *Railroads and Regulation;* and MacAvoy, *Economic Effects of Regulation.*

the rate structure. The ICC sanctioned what came to be called "value-of-service" pricing, wherein shippers with higher demand elasticities for service received lower rates. This is consistent with monopoly pricing, but it is also consistent with other pricing policies. The basic idea, however, is clear: pricing under this principle depends to some degree on what the market will bear instead of on the cost of providing the service. In the case of freight commodities, at a given transportation rate, the more valuable the commodity is per ton, the smaller the fraction of total delivered costs attributable to transportation. That, in turn, means that a given variation in transportation rates will have less effect on total delivered costs for high-value than for low-value commodities. For that reason, value-of-service pricing for freight transportation is thought of as equivalent to value-of-commodity pricing, wherein the rate per ton charged for a high-value commodity is higher than the rate for a low-value commodity, even if transportation costs are the same.

Since value-of-service pricing did not violate any of the discrimination provisions of the 1887 act or its amendments, and because it was a very attractive way of increasing rail profitability, the ICC sanctioned it, to the great benefit of the railroads. As pointed out by Friedlaender, this policy was also politically attractive: it pleased the vocal farm movement, because most agricultural commodities (such as grain) are low in value per ton, and hence value-of-commodity pricing meant relatively low rates for farmers.[12]

The policies resulting from the 1887 act and its pre–World War I amendments worked well politically as long as the railroad industry had a virtual monopoly. But with the advent of highway, barge, and air transportation, regulation designed to function under a rail monopoly had to adapt. The story of regulatory policies from 1920 to the present indicates continuous and generally inadequate attempts to do so.

The Transportation Act of 1920

During World War I the federal government took over the operation of the railroads. When it was over, Congress worked out legislation returning the industry to private ownership. The Transportation Act of

12. Ann F. Friedlaender, *The Dilemma of Freight Transport Regulation* (Brookings Institution, 1969), chap. 2.

1920 not only did this, but it also amended the 1887 act to broaden the ICC's powers significantly.[13]

Both testimony leading to this legislation and the provisions of the act indicate concern that returning the railroad industry to private ownership might make it infeasible to operate the nation's existing rail network profitably. The legislation seems an attempt to reconcile two conflicting objectives: maintaining an adequate return to rail investors and at the same time maintaining common carrier service obligations in the nation's rail system despite increased motor and barge competition. It did this in several ways.

First, it specifically allowed the ICC to set minimum rates. Even if rate wars had been avoided without these controls, their implementation virtually assured the absence of such wars.

Second, it transferred the control of entry into and exit from rail routes (through the chartering mechanism) from the states to the Interstate Commerce Commission. It is important to emphasize here that the 1920 act was not the first set of controls on entry and abandonments, as is sometimes argued. The states enforced this through charters, and until 1920 the charters may be thought of as representing rigid barriers to abandonment (to this day state governments are fervently opposed to abandonments). If anything, then, the 1920 act liberalized abandonment policies by allowing the ICC to overturn state charters and permit abandonments. Nevertheless, the ICC's policies toward abandonments generally supported the common carrier service obligations embodied in state charters and common law: carriers were often required to continue unprofitable services on the grounds that the public convenience and necessity required them. And of course, on the other side, allowing the ICC to control entry into the industry could help to keep competition out and to keep rates high where high rates were consistent with ICC goals.

Third, the 1920 act gave the ICC the right to promote mergers among railroads. There was a widespread view in Congress and among academics that a number of weak railroads would not be able to survive on their own, but that it was nevertheless politically and economically necessary to keep these lines in service with minimal public subsidies. So forced consolidations and consequent cross-subsidies were thought an appro-

---

13. A complete description of the Transportation Act of 1920 can be found in Daggett, *Principles of Inland Transportation,* chap. 29.

priate means of maintaining common carrier obligations without direct subsidies.

Fourth, if indirect or cross-subsidies were found to be inadequate for continued operation, the 1920 act also provided for direct subsidies in the form of guaranteed loans to weaker railroads.

Overall, then, the 1920 act tightened the ICC's cartel-like control over railroad rates to enhance profitability, and at the same time increased the ICC's powers to continue the operation of a rail system larger than an unregulated market would support in the face of growing competition from other modes.

Regulating Competing Modes

The Interstate Commerce Commission set about its obligations under the 1920 act to force large mergers on the railroad industry, commissioning Professor William Z. Ripley of Harvard University to develop a detailed merger plan redrawing the nation's railroad map. After considerable work, he came up with such a plan, but since it proposed to consolidate unprofitable railroads with profitable ones, the profitable ones (and some other parties) found it objectionable. Because of the problems it encountered, the ICC dropped its efforts to forcibly consolidate the nation's rail system.[14]

If mergers appeared to offer little help in staving off the decline of the railroad industry caused by highway competition, direct control of highway competition appeared to be a much more promising approach. As truck competition increased with the development of a paved national road system in the 1920s and 1930s, the railroads clamored more and more loudly for placing the trucking industry under the same regulation they were subject to.

This resulted in the Motor Carrier Act of 1935, which gave the ICC control of truck rates and entry. The ICC's power was increased by the Transportation Act of 1940, which brought certain barge transportation under the control of ICC regulation. Both motor and barge transportation, however, enjoyed considerable exemptions from regulation not afforded the railroad industry. All motor carriers of agricultural commodities were exempt from regulation, as were all water carriers of bulk

14. Ibid., chap. 24.

commodities so long as a single vessel or tow of barges contained no more than three distinct commodities. The 1940 act also made some changes (which turned out to be important) in rate regulation for the modes and commodities that were regulated. First, in an apparent attempt at further cartelization, in a case in which a carrier proposed a rate reduction the act placed the burden of proof that such a rate was "reasonable" on that carrier, rather than requiring anyone objecting to the reduction to prove the rate "unreasonable." The 1940 act also amended the Interstate Commerce Act by adding a preamble, labeled the National Transportation Policy. Under these provisions the ICC was to pursue regulatory policies that would create a transportation system adequate to the needs of commerce, defense, and the postal system, and that would bring about "sound economic conditions" among the carriers. On the other hand, it also stated that these conditions were not to be used by the ICC to keep the rates of one mode high to protect the traffic of another.[15]

The final legislation aimed at reducing competition was the Reed-Bullwinkle Act, passed in 1948. This legislation sanctioned rate bureaus for rail and truck transportation, which were basically cartelized rate-setting groups that the railroads had employed consistently since the nineteenth century, quite possibly in violation of antitrust laws.

As the 1950s began, an observer might well have believed that the railroads, and for that matter other transportation carriers, would find much to please them in public policies toward their industries. The cartelization that the regulatory process had been trying to achieve with the railroads was complete, protected by liberal antitrust exemptions. The value-of-service rate structure could be preserved intact, because all common carrier motor transportation carrying freight with high rates (more valuable manufactures) was subject to ICC regulation, with the explicit aim of controlling competition. Rate wars could be averted with exceedingly rigid safeguards against rate reductions. This combination of regulations and institutions should have pleased not only the railroads and truckers, but also the government policymakers who stood to gain from protecting weak routes with profits from stronger ones—high profits and a cartelized industry, one might have thought, should have enhanced the industry's ability to provide services.

---

15. George W. Hilton, *The Transportation Act of 1958: A Decade of Experience* (Indiana University Press, 1969), p. 9. This section has benefited from the work of Hilton.

Though regulation should at long last have "worked" for both railroads and policymakers in the 1950s, things did not turn out that way. Trucking proved to be a much more formidable competitor, especially in carrying high-value manufactured commodities, than many had imagined possible. In retrospect, this is not surprising. Because rail shipments must go through yards between trains, door-to-door delivery times tend to be slow and schedule unreliability is a serious problem (trains may run on time, but it is much more difficult to get cars through yards on time). Furthermore, the jostling that cars take in yards and from trains taking up "slack" when they start, plus the difficulty of policing rail operations against vandalism, make freight transported by rail much more subject to loss and damage than freight transported by truck. Slow, unreliable, and damage-prone transportation is most costly for high-value manufactured goods. Hence, even if the truck rate is considerably higher than the rail rate, high-value manufactured commodities are more likely to go by truck.

The relative advantage of truck transportation over rail after World War II was thus considerable, but since such goods as rubber and petroleum were tightly rationed during the war, the development of truck transport had been suppressed during that period. Other things increased the advantages of trucks over rail even more, including the rapid development of a much-improved highway system and the location of more and more manufacturing plants away from railroad sidings, which made rail terminal operations slower and more costly but were no disadvantage for trucks.

As a result, during the late 1940s, the 1950s, and the 1960s, the railroads found themselves losing more and more of their high-value traffic to truck transportation. And improvements in the waterways system plus unregulated barge competitors caused them to lose some bulk commodity traffic to barges as well.

Although the railroads made some technological efforts to compete with other modes, such as piggyback, or trailer-on-flatcar, transportation, their main response in the 1940s and 1950s was to reduce rates to counter the better truck service and the lower barge rates. The railroads, however, found themselves caught in the very regulatory web they had helped to spin: the ICC frequently blocked railroad rate cuts on the grounds that they were "unreasonable." Even if the rates exceeded the variable costs of railroads, and hence could potentially contribute to profitability, the commission nevertheless blocked many cuts, giving more often than not two reasons. First, it was feared that they could trigger a railroad rate war, thereby undermining the profitability of the railroad industry. The idea here was that variable costs were below average costs, and if all rates went to variable costs, it would bankrupt the industry. Second, potentially rate cuts could divert traffic from trucks and barges, thereby undermining the profitability of those carriers. Highway and water carriers had of course by this time developed a vested interest in regulation, because it often maintained rates at levels highly profitable to them.

Whatever the reasons were for these regulatory policies, the rail carriers did not like them. For the first time in history, the managements of more and more railways felt that more competition, rather than more regulation, offered them greater potential for economic gain. They wanted greater freedom not only to set rates, but also to abandon money-losing routes and services. At the time, money-losing passenger trains were viewed as the most onerous burden, those trains having lost most of their traffic to air and automobile transportation. So as a result of intermodal competition, the railroads wanted out of both common carrier obligations.

In the mid-1950s the railroads started an intensive lobby for more rate-making freedom. Their case was helped by the fact that, as the 1950s progressed, rail finances deteriorated, and they were especially hard-hit by the 1958 recession. Under these circumstances the lobbying paid off: it resulted in the Transportation Act of 1958, which was geared in several ways toward making ICC regulation both more supportive of competition and more favorable to the railroads.

First, the Transportation Act of 1940 was amended to state, as the railroads requested, that "rates of a carrier shall not be held up to a particular level to protect the traffic of any other mode of transportation." However, because of intensive efforts by the trucking and barge lobbies, this was to be done "giving due consideration to the objectives of the national transportation policy."[16] That is, consideration was to be given to the objective of preserving sound economic conditions among all the modes. Despite the ambiguities introduced by the truck and barge operators, the railroads regarded this as something of a victory.

Second, it allowed for guaranteed loans to railroads. This was to help financially troubled carriers rebuild their plants and equipment.

16. Ibid., p. 33.

Third, it brought the power to grant discontinuance of passenger trains under the ICC. Before that time, passenger train service had been regulated exclusively by the states and their regulatory agencies, again because the service had been provided by state charter and hence the states could require its continuation until they were willing to overturn the rail charters. By 1958 the rail passenger deficit had become, in the eyes of the railroads, an intolerable burden, equaling 40 percent of net freight operating income that year.[17] Yet state regulatory agencies often required continuation of passenger trains regardless of the size of the deficits involved. Under the Transportation Act of 1958, a railroad could discontinue an interstate train if that train was found to be no longer required for public convenience and necessity, *or* if its deficits were found to be an undue burden on interstate commerce. Discontinuing an intrastate train required that it meet both of those criteria.

Other sections of the bill related to trucking, of, at most, indirect concern to railroads; and with making interstate and intrastate rail rates consistent and not discriminatory.

The Transportation Act of 1958 did have some impact on regulatory decisions. In a number of cases the ICC allowed rail rate cuts despite the protests of truckers. Yet it also blocked some rail rate cuts, especially some that would have harmed the interests of barge operators. The railroads generally appealed these decisions to the courts, however, and though the process was lengthy and costly for the railroads, they got court approval for all but one of the desired cuts, the exception being the infamous 1965 Ingot Molds case.[18] In any event, as pointed out by a commissioner in 1957, the fraction of rail revenues at stake in these minimum rate proceedings was infinitesimally small.[19] In short, for rail rate-making freedom, the 1958 act was helpful in promoting competition and allowing rate cuts.

The same can be said about passenger train discontinuance. Many hopeless trains that state authorities had forced the railroads to keep in operation before 1958 the ICC now allowed the railroads to discontinue more or less immediately on application. Yet the commission still

17. Ibid., p. 36. The railroads, however, probably worsened their passenger problems considerably by investing in and emphasizing service on long-haul passenger routes—services that had been made obsolete by air transportation shortly after World War II. See Theodore E. Keeler, "The Economics of Passenger Trains," *Journal of Business*, vol. 44 (April 1971), pp. 148–74.

18. Hilton, *The Transportation Act of 1958*, pp. 74–78.

19. Ibid., p. 29.

required that a number of clearly unprofitable trains that were serious drains on rail finances be kept running, on the grounds that the public convenience and necessity required it. An extreme example of this was the proposal by the New Haven Railroad to discontinue all its intercity passenger trains. As table 1-2 indicated, the New Haven was not doing well financially at the time (in fact, it was bankrupt)—although it was losing a considerable amount on its passenger trains, the ICC refused to allow discontinuance.

The provision of the 1958 act allowing federal guaranteed loans was used to prop up weak railroads such as the New Haven, the Erie-Lackawanna, and the Lehigh Valley. It is difficult to argue that doing so made economic sense, but to the extent that there was a political demand for the services provided by these railroads, it is easy to see their purpose.

The effects of the act are fairly simple to summarize. It marginally increased the use of market forces to determine the allocation of resources in rail transportation. To the extent that guaranteed loans represent a modest subsidy (they do if one assumes that private lenders would have charged a higher interest rate if willing to lend at all), the act made a modest move toward replacing cross-subsidization with direct subsidization of money-losing services.

In the late 1960s and early 1970s the railroads got relief from both passenger service and minimum-rate regulation, but from very different sources. Passenger service was for the most part taken over by Amtrak, and although the railroads had to pay significant amounts to turn service over to Amtrak and although Amtrak probably does not fully compensate railroads for all services used, nevertheless it offered most railroads eventual relief from almost all their passenger burdens.

Relief on rates came from something not planned in the regulatory process: inflation. Since the consumer price index rose by nearly 50 percent between 1967 and 1974[20] and fuel costs by much more than that, the railroads could over that period easily achieve any effective rate cuts they might want for most commodities simply by failing to raise rates or not raising them as rapidly as costs went up. It is therefore not surprising that in the 1970s the railroads complained hardly at all about minimum-rate regulation. Suddenly the important constraint was not minimum rates but ICC controls on maximum rates.

20. *Economic Report of the President, January 1981*, p. 289.

The railroads' impetus for rate increases came not only from inflation and the ICC's delay in granting such increases, but also from an increased demand for the commodities that could most advantageously be moved by rail: grain and coal. Shifts in international prices and demand caused significant upward jumps both in these commodities' prices and in the demand for their transportation. It is no wonder that railroads in a position to carry these goods (and others for which they had similar advantages) sought rate increases that shippers tried to block.

The railroads were discontented with the size of the rate increases allowed and lobbied intensively for legislation that would allow the increases they wanted. At the same time, in the 1970s the financial situation of many railroads deteriorated. The Penn Central went bankrupt in 1970 and ran out of cash in 1976. Other railroads in the Northeast, including the Erie-Lackawanna, the Lehigh Valley, the Reading, and the Central of New Jersey, were also bankrupt.

To avoid running out of cash, the Penn Central petitioned the ICC in the early 1970s to be allowed to abandon 9,000 miles of road. This was refused, even though obviously the Penn Central was being forced to provide service on many highly unprofitable routes.[21]

It had become evident by the early 1970s that more legislation was urgently needed for the railroad industry. First, it would have to give the railroads more freedom to raise rates. Second, it would have to expedite proceedings for abandonment of unprofitable freight routes and services. Third, it would have to set forth a procedure for government takeover or subsidy of rail freight services that the market could not support but that were believed politically necessary. The last of these was especially urgent for Penn Central.

Overall, the 1970s saw the most dramatic changes in public policies toward rail transportation since 1887. These started with the formation of Amtrak in 1971 and continued with the Regional Rail Reorganization (3R) Act of 1973, the Railroad Revitalization and Regulatory Reform (4R) Act of 1976, and the Staggers Rail Act of 1980. Discussion of the Staggers Act will be presented in a later chapter.

The Regional Rail Reorganization Act of 1973

By 1973 the Penn Central, bankrupt for three years, was not only running out of the cash needed to meet its payrolls but was also suffering

21. "Penn Central: What Price Government Aid?" *Railway Age*, vol. 174 (February 12, 1973), pp. 10–11.

from severe physical neglect. It was evident that the federal government faced some difficult choices concerning northeastern railroads. Either government subsidies would be necessary or service would have to be cut back so drastically that a very large fraction of the rail shippers in the Northeast would be without service. After considerable debate, the 3R Act was passed.

The act established an agency, the Railway Association, to plan the reorganization and transition to public ownership of railroads in the Northeast. Based on economic and social criteria, it was to determine what parts of the northeastern rail system were worth keeping, and to recommend how much money in federal grants and loans was required both to operate the system in the near future and to rebuild and revitalize it to make it self-sustaining. It also set up a program for subsidizing low-density and other unprofitable service (especially that provided by bankrupt roads) outside the Northeast.

As a result of the Railway Association's recommendations, the publicly owned corporation, Conrail, arising from the Penn Central and several other bankrupt roads in the Northeast, contained 3,000 route-miles less than its parent lines. Conrail received federal subsidies of roughly $4 billion in its first five years of existence, from 1976 through 1981.[22]

The Railroad Revitalization and Regulatory Reform Act of 1976

By 1976 it was evident that the railroad problem went well beyond the Northeast. The Rock Island and the Milwaukee were nearing bankruptcy, the Katy was bankrupt, and the rest of the industry was earning a return on investment below what would be needed to keep it in existence at anywhere near its existing size.

All these considerations resulted in the 4R Act.[23] As the title implies, it had two aims: providing government subsidies and reforming regulation. Combination of the two goals in one bill showed at least an implicit awareness that they were interrelated, and if the federal government pursued both, it should do so consistently.

22. Congressional Budget Office, *Reducing the Federal Budget: Strategies and Examples, Fiscal Years 1982–86* (Government Printing Office, 1981), p. 81.

23. The provisions of the act are summarized and analyzed in Brock Adams, *A Prospectus for Change in the Railroad Freight Industry* (U.S. Department of Transportation, 1979), chaps. 6 and 7.

The portion of the act dealing with regulatory reform was geared to giving railroads more commercial freedom in several directions. These include rates, abandonments, and mergers.

On rates, the act contained several sections broadening the freedom of railroad firms. First, it settled the issue of minimum rates more clearly than the 1958 act had, indicating that no rate above variable costs should be considered unreasonable unless someone contesting it could prove otherwise. Second, it stated that the ICC should seek out types of traffic where rail transportation had no monopoly power and totally eliminate regulation there. Third, in rates as in proceedings, the commission was instructed to take the financial health of the railroad industry into consideration. This was intended to imply that any firm not earning a compensatory return on investment should be allowed to raise rates. Fourth, for areas in which a railroad firm was found not to have "market dominance," it was to be free to move its rates up or down within a 7 percent "zone of reasonableness" with no regulatory approval.

For mergers, the act shortened the time period within which the ICC must deal with a merger application and directed the secretary of transportation to facilitate mergers and other coordination projects. This provision, reminiscent of the Transportation Act of 1920, is discussed below, where separate consideration is given to policies toward rail mergers.

Concerning abandonments, the act established the principle that a railroad cannot be forced to provide service on which it loses money (and costs in this case are specified to include a return on investment). It too set a limit on the length of time during which regulatory deliberations could take place, in an attempt to make it easier and less costly for railroads to pursue abandonments. Also, it specified that efforts should be made to get shippers requiring the service under consideration to pay for it, through rate increases or possibly by forming separate shipper-owned companies to furnish the service. As a final incentive, the act provided subsidy appropriations for low-density lines of which the ICC had approved abandonment, but on which local authorities judged (and could prove to the Department of Transportation) that continued service was essential.

The subsidy program embodied in the 1976 act provided more than $500 million over a four-year period to subsidize money-losing branch lines, $600 million in grants for the rehabilitation of main lines for financially weak railroads, $1 billion in guaranteed loans for the same purpose, $1.75 billion to upgrade Amtrak's Boston–Washington route, and $2.1 billion in subsidies for Conrail (all subsidies were to be spent in the 1976–80 period).

In addition to these substantive policy changes, the act directed those charged with regulating and subsidizing the railroad industry to improve their information about both the needs of the industry and the effectiveness of their policies. It instructed the Department of Transportation to make a massive study of the industry's needs and problems and of the public policy changes needed to solve these problems, and it directed the Interstate Commerce Commission to develop a new costing methodology designed both to get a clearer idea of how costs varied with output and to better measure the industry's cost of capital.

Although the 1976 act contains many seemingly unrelated provisions covering the railroad industry, there is a logical unity to all its parts. Basically, the act shows an awareness that by the 1970s the railroad industry had long since ceased to be profitable enough to support all its existing money-losing common carrier obligations with profits from other services. Therefore, the rate regulation intended partly to provide such internal subsidization was eased, as was the common carrier obligation to furnish service on money-losing routes. The act also reflects the view that the public interest could best be served by allowing the industry to earn a "healthier" profit on services that were economically viable, in hopes that the physical plant for these services would be kept up by the private sector and would not require public support.

A more detailed economic analysis of these changes and of the goals for public policy they entail will be provided in subsequent chapters. For now I note only that neither the railroads nor those responsible for federal policy were satisfied with the effects of the 4R Act.[24] On the one hand, rail bankruptcies continued and Conrail continued to lose much money; and on the other, the ICC emasculated the provision giving railroads 7 percent flexibility in rates for traffic in which railroads had no market dominance, arguing that practically anywhere the industry has the discretionary power to raise rates in this way it has such dominance. The courts upheld the commission on this.[25]

The studies that the secretary of transportation was ordered by the

24. Adams, *Prospectus for Change*. This was a detailed Department of Transportation analysis, ordered by the 4R Act, of further legislative changes that would be needed in rail regulation, and the reasons these changes were necessary.

25. Ibid., pp. 120–21.

1976 act to make concluded that railroads were in worse shape than ever, with $3 billion to $6 billion in deferred maintenance in their plants, and that additional rate-making freedom (especially in the upward direction) was needed.[26]

Mergers

Many railroad mergers occurred in the nineteenth century before the passage of the Sherman Antitrust Act in 1889, but relatively few between 1909, when the Burlington–Great Northern Pacific merger was blocked, and 1956. Probably the most important reason is that in the 1920s and 1930s the ICC, at the request of Congress, developed merger plans that were unattractive to railroads. These plans required that profitable railroads buy less profitable ones, in a straightforward effort on the part of the federal government to promote further cross-subsidization of weak railroads. Without incentives to promote these plans, the railroads ignored them.

The Transportation Act of 1940 once again gave the ICC the power to grant rail mergers on a case-by-case basis, without reference to a grand scheme. Portions of this act (as it amends the earlier acts) require the commission to consider the effects of mergers on competition, as do the Sherman and Clayton antitrust acts for other firms, but also require that the ICC take into account the potential benefits of the proposed merger to shippers and travelers.

From 1956 through 1971 there was a steady stream of merger applications before the ICC. These included both parallel mergers (combination of two lines serving the same two end points), end-to-end mergers, and mixtures of the two. The ICC's policies toward these mergers were lenient. Of fourteen mergers applied for between 1956 and 1971, the ICC granted ten and refused two, and two were withdrawn by the carriers before decisions were made.[27]

A casual examination of this record makes it seem that there is little to learn about ICC policies toward rail mergers in the 1950s and 1960s. This is, first, because the two mergers that were blocked represent anomalous cases. The Frisco–Central of Georgia case, an end-to-end proposal, seems to have set no precedent, because after rejecting that

26. Ibid., p. 65.
27. Ibid., pp. 90–93.

merger the ICC allowed the much larger and more powerful Southern Railroad to buy the Central of Georgia instead of the Frisco. The decision to block the acquisition of the Western Pacific by the Southern Pacific, on the other hand, made sense on competitive grounds, because not only would it have created a monopoly between Salt Lake City and Oakland, but also it would have given control of the Utah-California lines to a carrier that could have had an incentive to divert traffic from them to a parallel line of its own to the south.

However, the mergers granted show a high level of permissiveness. Large parallel mergers, giving rail monopolies or near monopolies to large regions of the country, were permitted, including the Seaboard Coast Line, the Burlington Northern (the merger denied in 1909), and the Penn Central. Although some of these mergers were among weak firms or entailed strong firms' buying up weaker ones (such as the Penn Central and the Baltimore and Ohio–Chesapeake and Ohio), a number of others were among well-off or moderately well-off firms (such as the Norfolk and Western–Wabash–Nickel Plate and the Seaboard Coast Line).

Overall, based on rather superficial evidence, it seems that by the mid to late 1960s the ICC would allow just about any railroad to merge that desired to do so and that the courts would not overturn such mergers. Closer examination of some cases, however, indicates that this is not true, and examination of certain aspects of two specific cases gives a clearer picture of the ICC's goals in approving or denying mergers.

Consider first the case of the Union Pacific's application to buy the Rock Island, with certain parts of the latter road to be sold off to the Southern Pacific (this is one of the cases withdrawn before the commission decided it). The Union Pacific wanted the Rock Island particularly for its lines from Chicago and Minneapolis to Omaha, where they connected with the Union Pacific's main line to various points on the West Coast. This proposal brought strenuous objections from the other five railroads connecting Chicago and Omaha. One, the Chicago and Northwestern, alleged itself to be so weak financially that diversion of its Union Pacific connecting traffic to the Rock Island could bankrupt it. Another railroad connecting the Midwest and the West Coast, the Santa Fe, also felt it would be adversely affected. The ICC effectively decided this case by leaving it undecided for nearly ten years, during which time the Rock Island deteriorated so badly that the Union Pacific finally withdrew the application.

From the Rock Island–Union Pacific case, it would appear that the ICC was deeply concerned about the need to preserve a considerable network of weak or marginal railroads. Apparently this was not based on a desire to preserve market competition, because in other cases, such as the Seaboard Coast Line, the Penn Central, and the Burlington Northern, the commission seemed ready to accept a degree of firm monopoly in a region much larger than that involved in the Rock Island–Union Pacific merger. The commission seemed concerned instead with preserving service on the weak roads that might have gone out of business had their connecting traffic to the Union Pacific been diverted. Spreading out the traffic among several weak railroads was a way of accomplishing this.

Preserving unprofitable service also turned out to be an important consideration in the commission's reaction to the Penn Central merger. In this case a condition for approval of the merger was that the merged road take in the New Haven, which was sustaining large losses right up to the time of the merger and showed little promise of making a profit.

The same goal of preserving the service of weak competitors can be found in the various protective conditions attached by the ICC to some of the mergers that it did approve. Thus in allowing the Burlington Northern merger, the commission required that the Milwaukee, an extremely weak competitor of the merged road, be given trackage rights over the Burlington Northern to such places as Portland, Oregon, and Billings, Montana, to enhance the Milwaukee's competitive position (the subsequent bankruptcy of the Milwaukee indicates that these conditions did not achieve their goal).

In short, if one looks closely at the ICC's merger policies in the 1950s and 1960s, there does appear to be a consistent underlying purpose of protecting the service provided by weak carriers rather than of preserving market competition in a region.

Abandonments

Someone superficially familiar with ICC regulation might think it has pursued a permissive policy toward railroad abandonments, too. From 1920 through 1969 the ICC allowed 63,332 miles of abandonments out of a total of 73,335 miles applied for.[28]

28. Association of American Railroads, *Yearbook of Railroad Facts* (Washington, D.C.: AAR, 1976), p. 48.

Yet a careful look at all ICC policies suggests that this is not the case. In 1920–76 the ICC did not usually approve abandonments unless practically all shippers and local governments along a line accepted them.[29] This is compatible with the notion that the ICC has felt itself charged with enforcing corporate charters to provide service consistent with the Transportation Act of 1920. This fact and the long and costly procedures involved in pursuing abandonments[30] have discouraged railroads from pursuing abandonments unless they were confident of approval.

Public regulation in 1920–76 was thus a much tighter constraint on railroad abandonments than statistics on the percentage of abandonments approved indicate. This is clearly documented by what happened in the early 1970s, when the Penn Central applied to abandon 5,000 route-miles of service and the ICC refused the request, evidently on political grounds, despite the carrier's obvious economic need for such an abandonment. Further documentation of the ICC's policies toward abandonments may be found in its merger policies of protecting service on the routes of weak railroads.

Overall, then, there is plenty of evidence that before 1976 the ICC would not allow route abandonments, even by failing carriers, if there was any significant protest from shippers or local governments. And if the case of Penn Central is relevant, it seems that these policies toward abandonments may have done significant financial harm to the carriers.

Rates for Car Hire

With the exception of a tiny amount of narrow-gauge track, all railroad track in the United States is of standard gauge (4 feet 8½ inches), and rail cars and locomotives are built to be interchangeable among rail firms. Because a large fraction of the freight shipped travels over more than one rail line, railroads must interchange freight cars freely.[31] The ICC controls (and has controlled since 1920) the rates that one railroad may charge another for freight cars. Until very recently the ICC did not allow

29. Robert G. Harris, "Economic Analysis of Light Density Rail Lines," *Logistics and Transportation Review*, vol. 16 (January 1980), pp. 3–29, especially p. 24.

30. Ibid., p. 24.

31. One study estimates that about 70 percent of all car-miles are interline shipments. Robert G. Harris and Clifford Winston, "The Potential Benefits of Rail Mergers: An Econometric Analysis of Network Effects and Service Quality," *Review of Economics and Statistics*, forthcoming.

rates for car rental to fluctuate with changes in supply and demand; this resulted in shortages of cars at times and gluts at other times. Although recent studies imply that market-determined rates for freight cars were sometimes above ICC rates and sometimes below them, there is evidence that the ICC held the rates that one railroad could charge another for cars below free market levels.[32] The reason for this is that private-car-lessor and short-line railroads found it profitable to enter the market for rental freight cars at rates considerably above those the ICC allowed one Class I railroad to charge another.

To the extent that this is true, the ICC seems to have used car rental rates, as well as merger policies, to protect the weak railroads at the expense of the strong ones by offering weak roads unable to buy all the cars they need the opportunity to use the cars of better-off railroads at rates below market levels. In support of this, one can find evidence of complaints from strong roads about weak ones' keeping their cars too long.

Labor Policies

Labor policies go well beyond regulation by the Interstate Commerce Commission, but they are an important part of public policies toward the railroad industry. Because the industry is at once declining and regarded by federal policymakers as "essential," it has had difficulty laying off workers and changing outmoded work practices.[33] When the industry announces a major change, organized labor threatens a nation-wide strike. Because of the essential nature of rail service, the legislative or the executive branch of the government has tended to block such a strike and on occasion has forced labor and management to submit to compulsory arbitration.

This process has afforded some progress on work rules and wages in

32. See, for example, J. Sumner, "Deregulation and Fleet Efficiency" (Washington, D.C.: Public Interest Economics Center, 1980); and G. C. Woodward and C. E. Philip, "Problems and Opportunities in the Regulated Market for Railroad Freight Cars" (Conrail, 1980).

33. The Florida East Coast Railway has, through a long and costly series of strikes, managed to eliminate union work rules and wages. Its crews work eight-hour days and are paid somewhat below the union scale. The Florida East Coast nevertheless manages to fill all its positions and is a highly profitable railroad. See Luther S. Miller, "Florida East Coast: We Have to Be Different," *Railway Age*, vol. 180 (November 26, 1979), pp. 26–30.

the railroad industry, but it has been exceedingly slow. It was not until the mid-1960s, thirty years after the advent of the diesel locomotive, that the railroads were able to eliminate firemen designated to shovel coal on steam locomotives. Even now, Amtrak must use firemen on its passenger trains, and crews of three to seven are required on freight trains for which crews of two should be adequate. Furthermore, freight train crews are paid for a full day's work for 100 miles of travel, even if that entails no more than two hours' work. Finally, there is evidence that not only train crews but overhead workers such as stenographers (unionized on railroads) receive higher wages than the prevailing free market wage levels for equivalent skills.[34]

Although these labor agreements were made as a result of public policies pursued outside the regulatory process, some costly "labor protection" controls are achieved within it. For example, when two railroads wish to merge, they often make concessions to get the backing of labor in regulatory proceedings for the merger. For instance, the Penn Central agreed that if any worker of the parent lines was laid off as a result of the merger, that worker would be paid at full-time rates, complete with wage increases and fringe benefits, to the age of sixty-five.

Thus, although much of public policy toward rail labor has gone on outside the regulatory process, it has significantly affected the industry, and it has worked mainly to preserve more positions at higher wages than the free market would have supported.

Taxation and Subsidy

Although in its infancy the railroad industry was heavily subsidized, not only in the United States, but in Europe and Japan as well, the railroads now complain that competing modes of transportation, including trucks, barges, and planes, receive considerable government subsidies in the form of facilities and rights-of-way for which they do not have to pay the full costs in user charges.[35] The railroads, on the other hand, until recently had to pay not only the full costs of their facilities and equipment, but also property taxes, and were the major sources of tax

34. Adams, *Prospectus for Change*, pp. 58–62.
35. Ibid., pp. 45–48. See also Fred L. Smith, "An Efficiency Assessment of the Highway User Charge System" (Association of American Railroads, 1980).

revenue for some states and localities. Many believe not only that these discriminatory policies exist, but that they are inefficient and have a detrimental effect on the railroad industry.

Patterns of Public Policy toward Rail Freight Transportation

By 1975 the railroad industry in the United States was about 150 years old. In view of the changes in the country and the industry over that period and the shifting balance of political power among consumers and producers of rail transportation and competing modes, one might expect few consistent patterns of public policy toward the industry. Yet there have been some remarkably consistent patterns, especially in the last fifty years.

Possibly the strongest element of these is the old notion that the railroads, as common carriers, should provide a number of services at a financial loss, with the understanding that the regulatory agency would attempt to make up that loss from cartelized rates on other services. This idea underlies the requirements that railroads charge large and small shippers the same rates, though the costs may differ, and that money-losing freight and passenger services be maintained. It also seems to underlie the commission's goal of protecting weak railroads in merger cases and through artificially low car-hire rates.

Besides protecting the interests of those using money-losing services, the ICC has protected various other producer and consumer interests at times. In allowing rate bureaus and sanctioning value-of-service pricing, the ICC promoted a rail rate-making cartel, eliminated rate wars, and increased profits and reduced risks for rail investors. When trucking and barge interests were brought into the cartel, the ICC attempted to protect them—to some degree at the expense of the railroads. Furthermore, public policy, mainly through labor laws and compulsory arbitration, has tried to protect rail labor from the effects of the decline in the industry, through restrictive work practices, uneconomic layoff provisions, and higher wages than the free market would support.

Such producer-protective policies appear to be at the expense of consumers and shippers. Yet when railroads have attempted to raise rates in recent years, ICC regulation has often blocked them, and it is in that area that some of the most controversial reforms have been recently implemented.

CHAPTER THREE

Competition, Natural Monopoly, and Scale Economies

WHEN DISCUSSING the railroad industry, the terms "competition" and "monopoly" are often tossed about loosely. Kolko states that railroad regulation came about in the late nineteenth century not because the railroads were too monopolistic, but because they were too competitive.[1] He is referring to the fact that regulation aided the railroads in preserving a cartel and preventing rate wars. But in even the simplest economic theory, what do "too monopolistic" and "too competitive" mean? Are they as inconsistent as Kolko indicates? Similarly, it is often said about the railroads in the last half of the twentieth century that the industry is no longer a monopoly because of the competition of highway, water, and air transportation.[2] While this statement may be true in a broad sense, it still does not address the issue of whether railroads represent a natural monopoly in the narrower sense of economic theory, that is, it does not make it clear whether the private market can or will generate an economically efficient solution. It is the existence of a natural monopoly in that sense that determines whether the railroad industry requires public intervention to be efficient.[3] Of course, public intervention might occur whether it were efficient or not. But it is best to clearly understand whether the structure of the railroad industry is or is not competitive in the economic sense of the term, and if it is not, just what

1. Gabriel Kolko, *Railroads and Regulation, 1877–1916* (Princeton University Press, 1965).
2. This is stated, for example, in the Staggers Rail Act of 1980 (49 U.S.C., sec. 10101a, note).
3. If firms' entry into and exit from the market are sufficiently easy, even a natural monopoly can achieve efficient results. See William J. Baumol, "Contestable Markets: An Uprising in the Theory of Industry Structure," *American Economic Review*, vol. 72 (March 1982), pp. 1–15.

the structure is. This boils down to the matter of scale economies relative to the size of markets for rail transportation.[4] There is a sizable amount of empirical evidence on this issue, but first, it is necessary and appropriate to review some basic economic theory.

Market Structure

The theory presented here is so basic that something like it can be found in introductory economics textbooks. Yet because elaborate theoretical studies and econometric analyses often fail to take account of this theory, it is worth reviewing. This and the next chapter will expand on it with both empirical evidence and theoretical refinement.

I start with the simple case wherein there is only one market for rail services in which potential rail firms can operate. In this case the market includes shipments of a single commodity between two cities, with no intermediate service. Output (Q) is the flow of shipments of the commodity per unit of time, and long-run unit costs, marginal and average ($LRMC$ and $LRAC$), are as shown in figure 3-1. The figure represents a natural monopoly. As the density of traffic flows on the route increases, the average cost to a single firm ($LRAC$) declines over the entire area under the demand curve (D). There is room for only one low-cost firm in this market.

For such a natural monopoly to exist, it must always be cheaper for a single firm to produce the relevant output than for two or more firms to produce it.[5] It is not necessary that the average cost curve be falling over the entire range of output under the demand curve, as shown in figure 3-1—it can be flat or even rise where it hits the demand curve. But in the last case, the average cost curve must have been falling over some lower levels of output; otherwise, the above-mentioned conditions for natural monopoly will not be met.

Figure 3-2 shows a potentially competitive market. Economies of route density are exhausted when a relatively small amount of the market

---

4. Scale economies and indivisibilities are only one category of problems causing market failure. See Francis M. Bator, "The Anatomy of Market Failure," *Quarterly Journal of Economics*, vol. 72 (August 1958), pp. 351–79.

5. This condition for natural monopoly is called "sub-additivity." See Robert D. Willig, "Multiproduct Technology and Market Structure," *American Economic Review*, vol. 69 (May 1979), p. 349.

Figure 3-1. A Natural Rail Monopoly

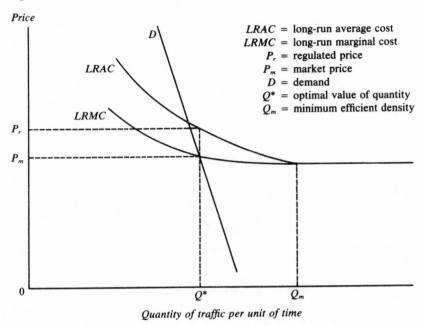

Quantity of traffic per unit of time

is accommodated. If there were free entry of firms into this market and if potential entrants had knowledge of the profits to be made and equal access to factor inputs, a competitive equilibrium would be achieved. In between the cases of "natural monopoly" and "naturally competitive" markets is the case of "natural oligopoly" wherein a small number of efficient firms will "fit" into the market.

Simplistic though such graphic representation is, it reveals some important things about the market for rail transportation that are often ignored.

First, these figures make it evident that economies of route density (the potential for lower costs as more traffic flows over a given route) are intimately connected with the potential existence of natural monopoly problems in the railroad industry. Although other economies of integrated operation are also relevant to the functioning of rail markets, any analysis of the potential for natural monopoly in transportation that fails to take account of economies of traffic density will not arrive at a logically correct resolution of the issue.

Second, the figures, combined with a rudimentary knowledge of

Figure 3-2. A Competitive Rail Market[a]

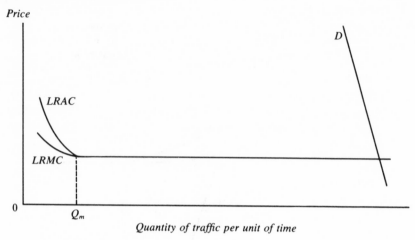

Price

Quantity of traffic per unit of time

a. See figure 3-1 for explanation of variables.

theories of oligopoly and competitive pricing,[6] offer a potential explanation for Kolko's statement that railroads were regulated because they
were too competitive rather than too monopolistic. Suppose that two
natural monopolists, having jointly entered a market, attempt to compete. Note that under these circumstances marginal cost (*LRMC*) for
each firm will be below average cost. Note also that if one firm cuts its
price but that price cut is not matched by the other firm, the price-cutting
firm will make money from any additional traffic won, so long as the
reduced price is still above marginal (not average) cost.[7] Unless collusion
is achieved, there will be a natural tendency for price to fall to marginal
cost. In a competitive industry this will produce a stable equilibrium,
because marginal and average costs are the same. In a natural monopoly,
however, marginal cost will be below average cost in the range of
production, since, as defined, the average cost curve falls through the
output range behind the demand curve. Thus when natural monopolies
try to compete, there is a distinct possibility of rate wars, characterized
by price cuts designed to avoid immediate matching by competitors. (It
is not surprising that, during nineteenth century rate wars, secret rate
kickbacks were often offered to large shippers.) This simple analysis can

6. This is, strictly speaking, Bertrand-type oligopoly behavior.
7. For a more elaborate discussion of the relationship between cutthroat competition
and excess capacity, see F. M. Scherer, *Industrial Market Structure and Economic
Performance* (Rand McNally, 1980), chap. 8.

easily be generalized to show that noncollusive, Bertrand-type pricing behavior will always result in losses as long as there are "too many" firms in an industry, for example, three entrants into a natural duopoly, and so forth.[8]

The outcome of this process, wherein excess capacity is driven out of a natural monopoly market, is often called destructive or cutthroat competition, because it could so easily cause at least one of the rivals to go bankrupt. Furthermore, once the rival was driven out, the incumbent firm could be expected to reap the full monopoly rents achievable from controlling the market. Recent theoretical developments, however, show that such outcomes do not necessarily hold.[9]

Consider the case of a natural monopoly market in which entry and exit are both easy and in which a new entrant is at no cost disadvantage. In this case, the loser in a fight such as this one, entailing destructive competition, can pull out easily before any significant losses are incurred and well before bankruptcy. So the loser is not nearly so badly off as in the story told above. But the winner is not so well off either. If it charges a price yielding any profits at all (beyond a normal return on capital), it will induce the entry of at least one other firm, and price rivalry will continue until all profits are eliminated—price will be driven down to average costs in the case of a single-product firm or to a welfare-maximizing combination of zero-profit prices in the case of a multiproduct firm (these are referred to in a later chapter as "second-best," or Ramsey, prices).

In short, Baumol and the others have documented that, with very easy entry and exit, a natural monopoly has almost all the attractive characteristics of a competitive market, eliminating the need for regulation. They appropriately call such a natural monopoly a "contestable" natural monopoly.

If railroads constituted a contestable natural monopoly, it would greatly simplify the task of regulating them, because the marketplace

---

8. Ibid.

9. A good summary of the literature on contestable markets is in Baumol, "Contestable Markets." Paradoxically, entry of new firms into natural monopolies can also cause market failure. See John C. Panzar and Robert D. Willig, "Free Entry and Sustainability of Natural Monopoly," *Bell Journal of Economics,* vol. 8 (Spring 1977), pp. 1–22. See also William J. Baumol, Elizabeth E. Bailey, and Robert D. Willig, "Weak Invisible Hand Theorems on the Sustainability of Multiproduct Natural Monopoly," *American Economic Review,* vol. 67 (June 1977), pp. 350–65; and William J. Baumol and John C. Panzar, *Contestable Markets and the Theory of Industry Structure* (Harcourt Brace Jovanovich, 1982).

could then be trusted to accomplish a large part, if not all, of the task of achieving efficient pricing and resource allocation in the industry. Common sense, however, indicates that the railroad industry is not contestable: entry entails a long and tedious process of buying up parcels of land, generally requiring powers of eminent domain (which, in turn, requires some government intervention). Engineering and building a railroad line also require considerable time and expense. So entry into the industry is anything but easy.

Exit is also difficult, largely because of public regulatory policies. But even without regulation, exit from the industry would be difficult by the standards of many other industries: heavy sunk costs, often financed with debt, are incurred to serve a specific market, without the opportunity to transfer them to other markets easily. While bridges, ballast, rails, and ties can be moved from one route to another, they can be moved only at great expense.

Overall, then, rail markets seem unlikely candidates for contestability. As firms are driven out of rail markets by rate wars, losing firms are likely, because of sunk costs, to go bankrupt rather than exit easily. And the entry of new firms into a given market should not be expected to be fast or easy.

Nevertheless, the theory of contestable markets is far from irrelevant to the railroad industry. A scheme wherein right-of-way was publicly owned, with privately owned locomotives and cars (and more than one firm competing on a given right-of-way), might allow contestable markets. Furthermore, to the extent that competing technologies, including trucks, barges, and coal slurry, have cost levels somewhere near rail costs, they may be able to impart to rail markets some of the characteristics of contestable markets.

The crude model of competition in the railroad industry just developed can, with one additional complication, be used to explain the Interstate Commerce Commission's concern with preserving weak carriers and preserving service on low-density lines. The analysis above assumes only service between two cities, with no intermediate service. But suppose that the abandonment of one of the railroads generated loss of service for intermediate cities not served by the other railroad. The ICC would then have a political incentive to try to maintain the first railroad, and indeed, there may be economic benefits to subsidizing it.[10]

10. Markets do fail when the demand curve hits the social average cost curve (or the cost curve for a single firm in a natural monopoly) where it is declining, so that the marginal cost is below the average cost. See Bator, "Anatomy of Market Failure."

Scale Economies

With a few exceptions, a railroad firm is likely to be larger and more complicated than the one discussed above. Specifically, it will probably haul a number of different types of commodities (with different costs) for different lengths of haul at different times between different points. And the overall size of the firm is likely to be quite independent of the amount of traffic that travels on a given route of that firm—that is, a large firm may have short or long hauls and high or low traffic densities between different points. Some commodity trips entail travel over high-density and low-density routes, with long and short trains.

Economies of route density can produce a natural monopoly on a given route, though in the absence of any other economies of scale, the national railway system could be made up of a large number of small firms, each with a local monopoly.

Another type of economy of firm integration that might be observed in the railroad industry is economies of length of haul. With fixed terminal expenses, longer hauls should mean lower costs per mile. If these economies exist, a railroad that has an integrated nationwide system will have an advantage over a railroad that must make and accept interline shipments to and from other railroads.

Still another type of scale economy is that of firm size. In rail transportation, economies of firm size would mean lower costs for larger firms, when length of haul and route density are held constant. If there were substantial economies of firm size without economies of traffic density, it would be economic to have a number of integrated nationwide (or international) railroads that competed on all their routes.

Finally, railroads, like most other modern corporations, are multi-product firms. Indeed, it is possible to view each different type of commodity trip (depending not only on commodity type, but also on the specific terminal points connected by the trip, on the time at which the shipment occurs, and on the quality of service) as a different product of the rail firm.[11] In the late 1970s a new literature developed on the theory

11. Transportation economists have been aware for some time that different passenger or commodity trips constitute very different types of output. See, for example, John R. Meyer, John F. Kain, and Martin Wohl, *The Urban Transportation Problem* (Harvard University Press, 1965), especially the appendix. The ICC has for some years estimated the costs of commodity trips using accounting procedures, but the only study to estimate

of multiproduct monopolies, which extended the relatively simple criteria for single-product natural monopoly to a somewhat more complicated set of criteria for multiproduct natural monopoly. For this analysis, it is important to take adequate account of this literature and of these criteria. However, the literature allowing rigorous testing of the hypothesis of multiproduct natural monopoly is not yet well developed, and most studies of scale economies in the industry have not been structured to adequately test the hypothesis of multiproduct monopoly.

Therefore, for the purposes of this study, I first survey most of the available literature on this topic from a single-product perspective, treating as the single product net ton-miles of freight hauled and assuming a commodity of "typical" weight, bulk, length of haul, and other characteristics. Once this survey is complete, I will present both a summary of the multiproduct theory and evidence on how my conclusions on natural monopoly in the industry can be affected by a more accurate multiproduct perspective.

Empirical Evidence on Scale Economies

In 1850 Dionysius Lardner wrote *Railway Economy: A Treatise on the New Art of Transport, Its Management, Prospects, and Regulations,* quite possibly the first systematic application of economic analysis to railroads. He set forth three basic principles of railroad economics, one of which was the following: "Railroad expenses do not vary in proportion to the volume of business handled."[12] In other words, Lardner asserted that rail transportation is subject to scale economies.

Ever since the time of Lardner, students of the railroad industry have debated whether there are scale economies in the industry.[13] Appendix B contains a critical survey of a number of studies on railroad costs conducted over the past thirty years. It shows that most of the studies

---

the costs of such commodity trips directly from an econometric cost function is Sergio Jara-Diaz and Clifford Winston, "Multiproduct Transportation Cost Functions: Scale and Scope in Railroad Operations" (Massachusetts Institute of Technology, April 1981).

12. Cited in Stuart Daggett, *Principles of Inland Transportation* (Harper, 1928), p. 53.

13. Indeed, the first statistical work on railroad costs was as early as 1916. M. O. Lorenz, "Cost and Value of Service in Railroad Ratemaking," *Quarterly Journal of Economics,* vol. 30 (February 1916), pp. 205–18.

conducted during the 1950s and 1960s found few economies of scale; they found that there were no economies of firm size and that economies of traffic density, if they were measured at all, appeared to be exhausted at very low traffic densities, so that practically all the main-line rail mileage in the country was operated subject to constant returns.

However, not everyone studying these matters agreed with this, and even those who did indicated some doubt. Meyer, Peck, Stenason, and Zwick, in one of the most important rail cost studies in the late 1950s, noted that the indivisibility of the rail plant was an important factor, making marginal and average costs different.[14] In general, studies that found constant returns to scale in the railroad industry suffered from methodological problems: they sometimes confused returns to firm size with returns to traffic density, or they allocated costs between freight and passenger service in questionable ways.

Studies of railroad costs from the 1970s tell a different but consistent story about returns to traffic density. They all give strong evidence of increasing returns, up to a rather high traffic density relative to tonnages moving over most route-mileage in the United States. These studies are based on differing econometric methods and specifications, although most are based on the same data set: larger Class I railroads in the United States for the late 1960s and early 1970s.

Some summary results of the analysis in appendix B are given in table 3-1, which shows the estimated percentage of costs that are variable (total revenues achievable through marginal cost pricing divided by total costs) evaluated at mean traffic density for each study, as well as estimated minimum efficient traffic density.[15] The table also indicates, where relevant, whether each study found increasing, decreasing, or constant returns to firm size when traffic density was held constant. Although there is a considerable variation in some of the figures shown in the table, it tells a reasonably consistent story.

First, consider the results on the percent of costs variable. Except for the Friedlaender and Spady study (for which the percent variable applies to high-density main-line trackage), all percent variables are evaluated at mean traffic densities for all firms in the sample. And the results of these studies are reasonably consistent—they indicate that, as of the

14. John R. Meyer, Merton J. Peck, John Stenason, and Charles Zwick, *The Economics of Competition in the Transportation Industries* (Harvard University Press, 1959), pp. 159–63.
15. For citations of all these studies, see appendix A.

Table 3-1. Some Evidence on Scale Economies from Cross Sectional Studies of U.S. Railroads[a]

Study	Year of study	Years of data set	Mean long-run cost elasticity (percent)	Minimum efficient density (millions of net tons)
Caves, Christensen,		1955	61.2[b]	n.a.
and Swanson	1981	1963	60.5[b]	n.a.
			71.6[b]	n.a.
Friedlaender and Spady	1981	1968–70	89.5	8.2
Harmatuck	1979	1968–70	51.7	7–8[c]
Harris	1977	1972–73	64	Over 30[d]
Keeler	1974	1968–70	57[e]	15
Sidhu, Charney, and Due	1977	1973	67	1.7

Sources: Douglas W. Caves, Laurits R. Christensen, and Joseph A. Swanson, "Productivity Growth, Scale Economies, and Capacity Utilization in U.S. Railroads, 1955–74," *American Economic Review*, vol. 71 (December 1981), pp. 994–1002; Ann F. Friedlaender and Richard H. Spady, *Freight Transport Regulation: Equity, Efficiency, and Competition in the Rail and Trucking Industries* (MIT Press, 1981); Donald J. Harmatuck, "A Policy-Sensitive Railway Cost Function," *Logistics and Transportation Review*, vol. 15 (May 1979), pp. 277–315; Robert G. Harris, "Rationalizing the Rail Freight Industry: A Case Study in Institutional Failure and Proposals for Reform," Sloan Working Paper 7705 (University of California at Berkeley, Department of Economics, September 1977); Theodore E. Keeler, "Railroad Costs, Returns to Scale, and Excess Capacity," *Review of Economics and Statistics*, vol. 56 (May 1974); and Nancy D. Sidhu, Alberta Charney, and John F. Due, "Cost Functions of Class II Railroads and the Viability of Light Traffic Density Railway Lines," *Quarterly Review of Economics and Business*, vol. 17 (Autumn 1977), pp. 7–24.

n.a. Not available.

a. All railroads are Class I (revenues of over $5 million a year in these years), except Sidhu, Charney, and Due, which are Class II short lines.

b. These are short-run cost elasticities, judged to be nearly equivalent to long-run cost elasticities in other studies. See appendix B.

c. These are the estimated densities at which 97.5 percent of costs are variable in the Harmatuck study. See appendix B.

d. In the Harris study 93 percent of costs are variable at 30 million net ton-miles per route-mile.

e. Referred to as a short-run elasticity in the Keeler study, but equivalent to a long-run function below minimum efficient density, as explained in appendix B.

late 1960s and early 1970s, on the average a railroad could recover 55 to 65 percent of its total costs with marginal cost pricing. As one might expect, however, all the studies found that as traffic densities rise, approaching minimum efficient density, the percent of costs variable rises. Thus in Harmatuck's study a doubling of the traffic density from the mean (roughly from 3.5 million to 7 million net ton-miles per route-mile) results in the percent of costs variable rising from 52 to 97.5. Similarly, Friedlaender and Spady's estimate of the percent of costs variable, because it imposes a large, discrete drop in costs between "low-density" and "high-density" lines, is most applicable to main-line operations with higher-than-average densities (see appendix B for a fuller explanation of this).

Properly interpreted, the evidence on cost elasticities seems to tell a consistent and reasonable story: for all but rather high-density main-line trackage, rail routes in this country operated at increasing returns to scale, with marginal costs below average costs. On the other hand, while a relatively large portion of the nation's route-mileage is the low-density sort, with marginal costs below average costs, relatively more of the traffic flows over higher-density routes, where this is not a problem.

Before considering this evidence on traffic densities, let us consider the evidence from the various studies on minimum efficient traffic density. As indicated in appendix B, estimates range from a low of 8 million to 10 million net ton-miles per route-mile (Friedlaender and Spady) to as much as over 30 million net ton-miles (Harmatuck, Harris). The cause of this seemingly distressing variation in results is not difficult to find; Friedlaender and Spady state it succinctly for all studies: "Since the standard errors of the coefficients . . . are large, and since one is extrapolating far beyond the sample range, these calculations [of minimum efficient density] may well be meaningless."[16] In other words, because the average route densities for most railroads are well below whatever the minimum efficient density may be, all calculations of minimum efficient density entail extrapolating along an estimated function. Naturally, under these circumstances, the estimates are likely to be quite sensitive to the specification of the cost function used. If this is so, one might be tempted to conclude that nothing can be said about minimum efficient density. Fortunately, the evidence contradicts this.

Specifically, in practically all studies the average cost curve starts to flatten out well before it reaches minimum efficient density, so that even if it is not completely flat within the observed range of traffic densities, it becomes almost flat. This is especially true of estimates based on the most sophisticated and flexible of functional forms, the translog function. Harmatuck found that at twice the mean traffic density in his study, equivalent to 7 million to 8 million net ton-miles per route-mile, 97.5 percent of costs were variable.[17] Similarly, Friedlaender and Spady found that for main-line operations of a number of large, high-density railroads almost all costs (95 to 100 percent) were variable. (Firms for which they found this to be true include the Santa Fe, the Missouri Pacific, the Southern Pacific, the Southern, and the Union Pacific.)[18]

16. Ann F. Friedlaender and Richard H. Spady, *Freight Transport Regulation: Equity, Efficiency, and Competition in the Rail and Trucking Industries* (MIT Press, 1981), p. 156.

17. Donald J. Harmatuck, "A Policy-Sensitive Railway Cost Function," *Logistics and Transportation Review*, vol. 15 (May 1979), pp. 303–04.

18. *Freight Transport Regulation*, p. 147.

Table 3-2. Freight Density for U.S. Line-Haul Railroads, Selected Years, 1929–80
Millions of net ton-miles per route-mile

Year	Freight density
1929	1.82
1939	1.44
1944	3.29
1950	n.a.
1960	n.a.
1970	3.74
1974	4.26
1979	5.02
1980	n.a.

Source: Calculated from Association of American Railroads, *Yearbook of Railroad Facts* (Washington, D.C.: AAR, 1981), pp. 36, 46.
n.a. Not available.

While the exact density at which railroad costs flatten out completely is not known, it is known that the cost curve for freight services becomes almost flat at around 7 million to 10 million net ton-miles per route-mile, depending on commodity type and other circumstances.

To determine the current importance of these economies of traffic densities in the railroad industry, table 3-2 looks at trends in those densities, and table 3-3 at recent estimates of those densities for various firms. As table 3-2 indicates, overall route densities have increased rather sharply in recent years, the mean value having risen by over 60 percent in the last decade (after many of these cost studies were completed) alone. Table 3-3, which presents traffic densities for individual railroads for 1969 and 1980, indicates even more clearly that some railroads, especially on their main lines, have probably reached or surpassed minimum efficient density for all practical purposes. But a large fraction of the nation's rail system operates at densities far below that. In 1975 fully 75 percent of the nation's rail network was operating below 8 million net ton-miles per route-mile.[19]

The studies discussed so far can best be interpreted as providing evidence on the long-run costs of rail services, with the route structure held constant (some of the results of Keeler and of Caves and others

19. Ibid., p. 220. Friedlaender and Spady's figures are in gross ton-miles per route-mile, but are equivalent to the figures mentioned in the text with a conversion factor of 2.6 gross ton-miles per net route-mile. See Robert G. Harris, "Rationalizing the Rail Freight Industry: A Case Study in Institutional Failure and Proposals for Reform," Sloan Working Paper 7705 (University of California at Berkeley, Department of Economics, September 1977), p. 52.

Table 3-3. Freight Densities of Major Railroads, 1969 and 1980

Millions of net ton-miles per route-mile

Railroad	1969	1980
Atchison, Topeka & Santa Fe	3.67	6.03
Baltimore & Ohio	5.29	4.46
Burlington Northern	2.61[a]	6.11
Chesapeake & Ohio	6.67	6.12
Chicago & Northwestern	1.63	3.10
Colorado & Southern	1.98	10.66
Denver & Rio Grande Western	4.26	5.97
Detroit, Toledo & Ironton	2.78	2.80
Fort Worth & Denver	1.10	6.55
Grand Trunk Western	3.05	3.49
Kansas City Southern	3.77	5.96
Louisville & Nashville	4.80	5.97
Marine Central	1.14	1.11
Missouri-Kansas-Texas	1.66	3.81
Missouri Pacific	2.98	5.01
Norfolk & Western	6.97	6.58[b]
Pittsburgh & Lake Erie	7.28	5.52[b]
St. Louis–Southwestern	5.74	7.75
Seaboard Coast Line	3.36	4.26
Soo Line	5.64	6.27[b]
Southern	4.22	5.35
Southern Pacific	5.64	6.27[b]
Union Pacific	4.91	7.87[b]
Western Maryland	4.11	1.80
Western Pacific	4.15	3.20

Sources: 1969 (or 1971) data, Interstate Commerce Commission, *Transport Statistics* (Government Printing Office, 1970, 1972); 1980 (or 1979) data, *Moody's Transportation Manual* (1981).
a. First entry for Burlington Northern is 1971.
b. Second entry for these railroads is 1979.

were described as short-run costs, but their short-run cost functions are best interpreted as long-run ones below minimum efficient density; see appendix B). Recently, however, there have been some important time series studies of short-run rail costs, including those of Braeutigam, Daughety, and Turnquist; Jara-Diaz and Winston; and Charney, Sidhu, and Due.[20] These studies are useful on three counts. First, they give some indication of the relationship between average and marginal costs

20. Ronald R. Braeutigam, Andrew F. Daughety, and Mark A. Turnquist, "The Estimation of a Hybrid Cost Function for a Railroad Firm," *Review of Economics and Statistics,* vol. 64 (August 1982), pp. 394–404; Jara-Diaz and Winston, "Multiproduct Transportation Cost Functions"; and Alberta H. Charney, Nancy D. Sidhu, and John F. Due, "Short Run Cost Functions for Class II Railroads," *Logistics and Transportation Review,* vol. 13 (December 1977), pp. 345–59.

Table 3-4. Evidence on Short-Run Rail Costs

Study	Year of study	Years of data set	Range of cost elasticities
Braeutigam, Daughety, and Turnquist	1980	1969–77	15.8
Charney, Sidhu, and Due	1977	1963–73	0–75
Friedlaender and Spady	1981	1968–70	58–150
Jara-Diaz and Winston	1981	1975–80	35.2–78.7[a]

Sources: Ronald R. Braeutigam, Andrew F. Daughety, and Mark A. Turnquist, "The Estimation of a Hybrid Cost Function for a Railroad Firm," *Review of Economics and Statistics*, vol. 64 (August 1982), pp. 401–02; Alberta H. Charney, Nancy H. Sidhu, and John F. Due, "Short Run Cost Functions for Class II Railroads," *Logistics and Transportation Review*, vol. 13 (December 1977), p. 352; Friedlaender and Spady, *Freight Transport Regulation*, p. 147; and Sergio Jara-Diaz and Clifford Winston, "Multiproduct Transportation Cost Functions: Scale and Scope in Railroad Operations" (Massachusetts Institute of Technology, April 1981).

a. These numbers are the reciprocals of Jara-Diaz and Winston's estimates of global scale economies, $\hat{S}_m$. Thus for firm 1, $\hat{S}_m = 1.27$. So the cost elasticities are $1/2.84 = 0.352$ and $1/1.27 = 0.787$, respectively.

for existing levels of investment in rail plant. Since many of these costs will be sunk for some time to come, it is useful to know what these short-run costs are. Second, because all these studies are based on highly disaggregated data for small firms, they give an idea of how aggregating data for cross sectional studies of larger firms has affected the results. Third, also because of their disaggregation to small firms with simple route networks, these studies allow the testing of other relatively specialized hypotheses about the nature of rail technology. Braeutigam and his colleagues, for example, analyze the impact of service quality (operating and yard-processing speed) on rail costs. Jara-Diaz and Winston test for the existence of multiproduct natural monopoly. (Once again, a more detailed discussion of all these studies may be found in appendix B.) The results of these studies, in terms of short-run cost elasticities, are presented in table 3-4. Also included in the table are the results of the only cross sectional study to analyze true short-run costs (that is, with both route structure and plant capital held constant), that of Friedlaender and Spady.

The results of the short-run cost studies are consistent on only one count—they show a wide range of variation in the percent of costs variable. As pointed out by Friedlaender and Spady, this is apparently because many poorer railroads have neglected their plants, making the marginal costs of using them relatively high. On the other hand, railroads that have maintained their plants well tend to have short-run cost elasticities at or below the equivalent long-run levels. The results of the disaggregated short-run studies also indicate that the cost characteristics of a shipment depend fairly heavily on the circumstances—the relevant gradients, commodity types, urbanization, and so forth. The more aggregative studies may not always be accurate about costs of specific shipments, although the importance of these effects is not known.

In summary, then, based on a single-product approximation, a large fraction of the nation's rail system operates subject to increasing returns to traffic density, while the more important main lines are more likely to operate at near-constant returns to traffic density.

The Nature and Causes of Scale Economies

For purposes of subsequent analysis, and especially to understand how generalization of the preceding analysis to a multiproduct framework would affect the results, it is useful to analyze the reasons for the existence of scale economies in the railroad industry.

For many years those who believed that there were economies of traffic density assumed that they stemmed from a high level of "fixed" costs, mainly the capital and maintenance expenses of road property. It could be argued that if this was true the problems of destructive competition should no longer exist if these costs were written off: the only remaining costs should then be ones that vary with the amount of traffic carried. Since the industry is a declining one, so the argument goes, it will never need to recover these written-off costs.

The main problem with this argument is that its premise—that scale economies in the industry derive exclusively from fixed capital costs— is untrue. Miller first noted in 1973 that a large part of the economies of density in the railroad industry derive from costs other than capital and maintenance costs of way and structures.[21] Specifically, he found that part of them come from line-haul operations, such as engine crew costs, and another part from equipment maintenance and capital costs.

Although at first this may seem strange, in fact it makes good sense. As traffic densities rise, trains tend to get longer, thereby reducing line-haul crew costs per ton of freight carried. Train frequencies also rise, and this allows for better utilization of both labor and equipment. All these things appear to cause significant economies of traffic density, at least below densities of 8 to 10 ton-miles per route-mile.

The evidence on economies of density that Miller first noted have

21. Edward Miller, "Economies of Scale in Railroading," *Proceedings—Fourteenth Annual Meeting, Transportation Research Forum,* vol. 14, no. 1 (1973), pp. 683–701.

since been confirmed by many subsequent studies, including those of Friedlaender and Spady, Harmatuck, Harris, and Keeler.[22]

However, to some degree the economies of traffic density observed here stem from restrictive work rules. The economies of operation for long trains arise largely because a train must generally have a crew of from three to seven, who are paid a full day's wage for only 100 miles of work. If the crew numbered only two and if they were paid lower, market-clearing wages, scale economies from long trains would be far less important.

Finally, economies of route density can take the form not only of lower costs, but also of better service at the same costs. If higher density allows a railroad to operate more frequent trains, it may not achieve lower costs, but it may well make more money because shippers value better service. Harris and Keeler confirm that whether it comes from better service or lower costs, a high route density contributes to a high level of profitability, all other things being equal.[23]

Scale Economies in a Multiproduct Framework

In recent years a substantial body of literature has developed on natural monopoly in a multiproduct setting. This literature shows that the criteria for natural monopoly in a multiproduct setting are considerably more complicated than the single-product criteria discussed so far in this chapter.[24]

Because little work has been done to empirically test the criteria for multiproduct natural monopoly in the railroad (or any other) industry, I

22. Friedlaender and Spady, *Freight Transport Regulation;* Harmatuck, "A Policy-Sensitive Railway Cost Function"; Harris, "Rationalizing the Rail Freight Industry"; and Theodore E. Keeler, "On the Economic Impact of Railroad Freight Regulation," Sloan Working Paper 7601 (University of California at Berkeley, Department of Economics, September 1976).

23. Robert G. Harris and Theodore E. Keeler, "Determinants of Railroad Profitability: An Econometric Study," in Kenneth D. Boyer and William G. Shepherd, eds., *Economic Regulation: Essays in Honor of James R. Nelson* (Michigan State University Press, 1981), pp. 37–54.

24. The references on this topic are numerous. See, for example, William J. Baumol, "On the Proper Cost Tests for Natural Monopoly in a Multiproduct Industry," *American Economic Review,* vol. 67 (December 1977), pp. 809–22. A useful summary of this literature may be found in Robert D. Willig, "Multiproduct Technology and Market Structure," *American Economic Review,* vol. 69 (May 1979, *Papers and Proceedings, 1978*), pp. 346–51.

cannot provide anything close to definitive evidence on the extent to which analysis in a multiproduct framework would affect the results. Nor is this the place for a detailed, technical discussion of the theoretical criteria for natural monopoly—that should be (and is) the subject of another book.[25] Nevertheless, I can provide a brief, nontechnical review of the criteria for multiproduct natural monopoly and summarize what evidence is available so far on the extent to which multiproduct analysis would change my results on railroads.

Although the technical criteria for natural monopoly with multiproduct firms can be complicated, the ideas behind these criteria are simple. At the most basic level, the criteria are the same for single- and multiple-product firms: for there to be a natural monopoly for a collection of goods and services, it must be cheaper for one firm to produce that collection than for more than one firm to produce it. But except for that similarity, the criteria for natural monopoly for multiproduct firms are much more complicated than for single-product firms.

For multiple-product firms, unlike single-product firms, there are several potential definitions of scale economies, no one of which is sufficient to assure the existence of natural monopoly. Two types of scale economies, however, when they occur together, are sufficient (though not necessary) to assure natural monopoly. The first of these, called product-specific economies of scale, are very like decreasing average costs for a single-product firm. To define them, the avoidable costs of one product (say, X) of a multiproduct firm are first defined as the costs that could be avoided if the firm's output of X went down to 0, when all other outputs are held constant at some given level. The average avoidable costs for some output level X are then total avoidable costs divided by that output level. A firm has product-specific economies of scale for product X if over all output levels for that product, and for all combinations of outputs for other products, there are declining average avoidable costs associated with increased outputs of X.

Unlike the case of a single-product firm, however, product-specific scale economies are not in themselves sufficient to guarantee natural monopoly in the case of multiproduct firms. This is easy to show intuitively. Consider the case of a railroad providing two products only, hauling freight and passengers between points A and B. Suppose total costs for the railroad are simply the sum of two separate cost functions,

25. William J. Baumol, John C. Panzar, and Robert D. Willig, *Multiproduct Technology and Market Structure* (Harcourt Brace Jovanovich, 1982).

each with marginal costs below average costs throughout all relevant ranges of output:

$$TC = F(P) + G(F),$$

where TC is total costs, P is passengers, and F is tons of freight. Such a market would tend to have separate natural monopolies in passenger and freight traffic, because there are product-specific scale economies in each. That is, a market combining all passenger services in one firm will have lower costs than a market with two passenger firms. The same is true of freight.

But these product-specific scale economies offer no incentive for aggregating both passenger and freight services under one firm. For a multiproduct natural monopoly to occur, it is necessary to have another type of economy, described by Panzar and Willig as economies of scope.[26] Essentially these represent economies of aggregation of the production of many services or goods under one firm.

A natural monopoly must have a combination of product-specific scale economies and economies of scope. (Just as scale economies alone are not sufficient for natural monopoly, so economies of scope alone will not allow it either—if there were only economies of scope and no scale economies, production could occur in many small, diversified firms.)

Because the empirical study of multiproduct natural monopoly is in its infancy, there is relatively little evidence on which to base any empirical conclusions. Only one study, that of Jara-Diaz and Winston, has been specified to test for the existence of multiproduct natural monopoly in the railroad industry, and it is based exclusively on a sample of tiny Class III railroads.[27] Nevertheless, its evidence is revealing. It shows that if one ignores the fixed maintenance and capital costs for way and structures, there are insufficient economies of scale and scope to cause natural monopoly in the industry. On the other hand, Jara-Diaz and Winston hypothesize that if these way-and-structures costs were included, there would be enough economies of scale and scope to guarantee natural monopoly at the low densities at which the Class III railroads in their sample operate. But they state that this result is tentative and subject to further confirmation.

In any event, Jara-Diaz and Winston's results are at least roughly

26. John C. Panzar and Robert D. Willig, "Economies of Scale in Multi-Output Production," *Quarterly Journal of Economics,* vol. 91 (August 1977), pp. 481–94.
27. "Multiproduct Transportation Cost Functions."

consistent with the following hypothesis: below the point at which a single-track main line is fully utilized, there are sufficient economies of scale and scope to guarantee natural monopoly. Beyond this point, the natural monopoly disappears. At least one study of the industry, dating from 1974 and hence preceding the literature on the multiproduct natural monopoly, was specified to yield this result.[28]

This makes good intuitive sense: at low densities, different types of freight share both trains (with more than one type of commodity on a train) and track. As more commodity types are carried on a given route, they are carried at lower costs, because the trains are longer and the tracks are better utilized. And as increases in any one commodity type allow for longer trains and better plant utilization, scale economies as well as economies of scope result.

Thus it is reasonable to believe that the same results hold in a multiproduct setting as in a single-product setting: below minimum efficient density, there are sufficient economies of scale and scope to guarantee natural monopoly. Beyond that level natural monopoly may no longer exist. However, in a multiproduct setting the concept of minimum efficient density is an ambiguous one: it could be, say, 7 million net ton-miles per route-mile for new automobiles, or 10 million net ton-miles per route-mile for coal, or some number in between for some given combination of autos and coal. Because the evidence based on multiproduct criteria is incomplete, these conclusions are tentative.

All the evidence presented here and in appendix B confirms the hypothesis of increasing returns to traffic density over most route-mileage in the railroad industry and, along with the simple model presented earlier in the chapter, suggests that scale economies are likely to play an important role in the railroad industry, both in the market behavior of the firms and in the regulatory policy of the government.

28. Theodore E. Keeler, "Railroad Costs, Returns to Scale, and Excess Capacity," *Review of Economics and Statistics*, vol. 56 (May 1974), pp. 201–08.

CHAPTER FOUR

The Effects of Rail Freight Regulation

THIS CHAPTER addresses two interrelated questions. First, what social goals are the regulatory policies trying to attain, and second, what have the economic effects of the policies been? The chapter first sets forth a conceptual framework for analysis of the causes and effects of these regulatory policies, and then provides empirical evidence as it relates to both the various hypotheses advanced and, more broadly, the benefits and costs of freight regulatory policies.

Two schools of thought have evolved on the economic theory of regulation. The older and more established of the two is normative: it is concerned with determining, both theoretically and empirically, the most efficient prices and outputs that could be achieved in an industry, and it provides a means of evaluating regulatory policy based on how close a regulated industry comes to achieving efficient prices and outputs. To the extent that regulators actually follow (or attempt to follow) economically efficient policies, this mode of analysis also contributes a positive theory of regulatory behavior; it has been dubbed the "public interest" theory of regulation.[1] The second school of thought is concerned only with explaining what regulators do, and it is based on the belief that economic efficiency is not the primary goal of regulators so that a valid theory of regulation must go beyond the public interest theory. Although many of the elements of this second group of theories were developed by political scientists, it has been worked out in economic terms by Stigler, Peltzman, Posner, and others at the University of Chicago.[2] For that reason, I refer to this group as the "Chicago" theory of regulation.

1. A summary of these theories may be found in Richard A. Posner, "Theories of Economic Regulation," *Bell Journal of Economics*, vol. 5 (Autumn 1974), pp. 335–58.
2. See George J. Stigler, "The Theory of Economic Regulation," *Bell Journal of Economics*, vol. 2 (Spring 1971), pp. 3–21; Richard A. Posner, "Taxation by Regulation,"

Both groups of theories will be useful for this study; it is certainly important to evaluate rail regulatory policies relative to the normative optimum of economic efficiency. But where existing policies diverge from efficient ones, it is equally important to know why, for only then can the feasibility of more efficient solutions be understood.

This study will therefore develop both positive and normative models of optimal regulatory policies toward the railroad industry. The models extend the theory of previous models of regulation by incorporating indivisibilities and the benefits of an extended route network in a new and simpler way. Also presented is a new, integrated model of regulatory behavior in which the Chicago and public interest theories are special cases.

A Simple Model of Efficient Regulation

It is most convenient to start with a simple normative model based on a single market for freight transportation. Figure 3-1 showed a case where there is room in the market for only one firm, and the demand curve hits that firm's average cost curve in its declining region, so that marginal cost is below average cost. The regulated price (received by the firm) should then be P_r, and the market price (paid by the shipper) should be P_m. To achieve maximum economic efficiency, the service should be subsidized by $P_r P_m$ for each unit of the commodity carried. On the other hand, if, as in figure 4-1, the demand curve hits the average cost curve beyond minimum efficient density, it will still be necessary to regulate the monopolist (at P_r), but no subsidy will be necessary. If there is room for more than one firm of minimum efficient scale in the market, the need for regulation depends on the extent to which firms manage to keep prices above costs through coordination—if they are unable to coordinate their pricing policies, competition will ensure that the price is driven toward marginal cost.

The simple model of natural monopoly in the railroad industry is suggestive, but more complete analytical models are necessary to derive positive and normative hypotheses about the industry. Appendix C

Bell Journal of Economics, vol. 2 (Spring 1971), pp. 22–50; Posner, "Theories of Economic Regulation"; and Sam Peltzman, "Toward a More General Theory of Regulation," *Journal of Law and Economics*, vol. 19 (August 1976), pp. 211–40.

Figure 4-1. A Natural Monopoly Requiring No Subsidy

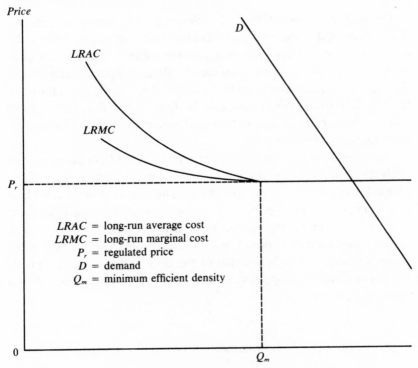

Quantity of traffic per unit of time

develops these models mathematically, stating as well all the assumptions underlying them, as briefly summarized here.

The simplest theoretical model discussed in appendix C is a straightforward extension of the graphic model of natural monopoly just given. It assumes that some shippers at least attach value to a larger national rail route system as well as to lower rates for a given commodity when the size of the route system is held constant. Not surprisingly, it shows that much trackage will be operated below minimum efficient traffic density, with the result that optimal pricing will lead to a loss.

There has been considerable evidence, however, that the American public is unwilling to subsidize transportation deficits on a large scale. For precisely this reason second-best pricing strategies have been developed that aim to maximize net benefits to consumers from a set of services provided, subject to the constraint that, overall, the services break even.

The goal of the model, then, is to derive a set of optimal commodity freight rates and a route network of optimal size, so as to maximize the net benefits of rail services in a country subject to the break-even constraint. These rates are often called "Ramsey prices," after Frank Ramsey, who originated them in the 1920s; their implications for regulatory policy were explored in detail by Baumol and Bradford in 1970; and they have been applied to transportation many times, for example, by Walters and Braeutigam.[3]

The second-best model developed in appendix C differs from previous analyses of second-best pricing in that it permits setting the optimal network size jointly with optimal prices. The results of the second-best model generate Ramsey prices, which, like monopoly prices, differ from marginal costs in inverse proportion to demand elasticities. However, except where monopoly prices generate zero profits, the overall level of Ramsey prices will be below that of monopoly prices, because prices needed to assure a competitive return will be below prices needed for a monopoly return.

Models for the Maximization of Political Support

The most sophisticated approach to the theory of regulation assumes that the regulator is interested not in achieving maximum public benefit, but rather in paying off those to whom he is most politically beholden.

---

3. F. P. Ramsey, "A Contribution to the Theory of Taxation," *Economic Journal*, vol. 37 (March 1927), pp. 47–61; William J. Baumol and David F. Bradford, "Optimal Deviations from Marginal Cost Pricing," *American Economic Review*, vol. 60 (June 1970), pp. 265–83; A. A. Walters, *The Economics of Road User Charges* (Johns Hopkins University Press, 1968); and Ronald R. Braeutigam, "Optimal Pricing with Intermodal Competition," *American Economic Review*, vol. 69 (March 1979), pp. 38–49. A regulator practicing second-best pricing for rail would ideally like to restrict entry and control rates in truck and barge transportation as well. This would generate a different set of rail rates from those derived here, based on cross-elasticities of demand between rail and truck transportation. This analysis (not covered here) has been worked out by Braeutigam ("Optimal Pricing") and analyzed empirically by Clifford Winston, "The Welfare Effects of ICC Rate Regulation Revisited," *Bell Journal of Economics*, vol. 12 (Spring 1981), pp. 232–44. While it is not known for certain what such intermodal second-best rates would be, evidence from Winston suggests that they would differ considerably from existing regulated rates.

Political scientists originated this; later Olson and Stigler developed its economic implications.[4] Stigler argued that there is a market for regulation through the political process, and for those ready to pay for it, the political system is ready to supply it. Stigler noted, for example, that the suppliers of goods and services (firms and factors of production) should have an incentive to purchase regulation because regulation can be used to block entry and raise prices, and hence profits and factor payments. Given these considerations, Stigler and others argued, it is little wonder that regulators (including the Interstate Commerce Commission) generally failed to pursue public interest goals such as overall economic efficiency.

As noted by Hilton, the ICC has had a consistent tendency to reward one group of users of rail services at the expense of others (cross-subsidization).[5] Posner suggested that this was consistent with Stigler's theory, but also noted that it constituted a form of fraud, because the redistribution of income that occurs with cross-subsidization by regulation can generally be achieved much more efficiently by direct taxation.[6] The only incentive to use cross-subsidization is that taxpayers are unaware of it.

Peltzman presented a general, formalized theory of regulation, extending the work of Stigler and Posner.[7] He postulated that the regulator maximizes a political support function, for which prices and service levels for different services and users are arguments. In fact, if firms that the regulator controls must abide by the break-even constraint, the regulator will endeavor to raise and lower prices of various services subject to that constraint so that his political support will be maximized. The result of the Peltzman model is that a dollar's worth of subsidy money directed to any user or factor should generate the same amount of political support on the margin. Peltzman shows, for example, how a regulator controlling a firm with both low-cost and high-cost users can increase political support by raising the price above marginal cost for low-cost users and lowering it for high-cost users.

4. Stigler, "Theory of Economic Regulation"; and Mancur Olson, *The Logic of Collective Action: Public Goods and the Theory of Groups* (Harvard University Press, 1965).

5. George W. Hilton, "The Basic Behavior of Regulatory Commissions," *American Economic Review*, vol. 62 (May 1972, *Papers and Proceedings, 1971*), pp. 47–54.

6. Posner, "Taxation by Regulation," and "Theories of Economic Regulation."

7. "Toward a More General Theory of Regulation."

An Integrated Model of the Chicago and Second-Best Theories

Appendix C presents the detailed derivation of a model of regulation for which the Chicago, "first-best," and second-best models of behavior are all special cases. This theory is developed by integrating Peltzman's model with the neoclassical theory of costs, production, and consumer preferences. It is further expanded by allowing for various potential route configurations, as in the case of the second-best theory above, so as to make it more consistent with the case of the railroad industry.

The results of this model indicate that a support-maximizing regulator will generally not allow Ramsey—or value-of-service—prices, the only exception being when a dollar's worth of consumer or producer surplus for all users and suppliers has the same political support attached to it.

On this count, however, it must be noted that a support-maximizing regulator as well as a public interest regulator will take scale economies into account. That is, the existence of scale economies, all other things being equal, will give the support-maximizing regulator an incentive to regulate, because they increase the consumer surplus that could be distributed to someone (and hence the political support) engendered by regulation.

To summarize the alternative hypotheses afforded by the theoretical models developed in appendix C, first-best policies (that is, long-run marginal cost prices) are likely to entail substantial losses for the railroad system and prices near what the ICC refers to as "variable" or "out-of-pocket" costs for all commodities. Second-best pricing, like monopoly pricing, would entail prices inversely correlated with demand elasticities. Prices for each market would be raised according to what that market would bear, but *only* to levels that would permit the firm to earn a competitive return on investment. In the absence of intermodal competition, this would bear some resemblance to a value-of-service pricing structure. If there is substantial intermodal competition, policies focusing on value-of-service pricing will generate low ratios of prices to costs for the commodities for which there is strong intermodal competition, but higher ratios for the goods for which shippers are captive (unless, as suggested by Braeutigam, competing modes are also regulated[8]).

8. Braeutigam, "Optimal Pricing," pp. 38–50.

These models generate testable hypotheses about regulatory behavior, so some inferences regarding the motivations of ICC regulation should be possible. The models generate such hypotheses in two areas, rates and route system size.

Rate Regulation

Economic studies of rail rates done in the 1950s and 1960s held that regulation kept rates high relative to marginal costs for high-value goods and lower for bulk commodities, along the traditional lines of value-of-service pricing.[9] Students of regulation at the time believed that minimum-rate regulation was the culprit preventing competition from driving the rates on high-value commodities down to marginal costs. There was indeed considerable evidence that the ICC attempted to keep rates on high-value commodities up in a number of cases.

Furthermore, to the extent that researchers in the 1950s and 1960s believed that scale economies in the railroad industry were unimportant,[10] it was also logical to believe that a combination of competition and regulation (restricted to captive shippers) could generate marginal cost (or near-marginal cost) prices for the railroad industry, so that marginal cost pricing provided an appropriate benchmark for comparison of actual with optimal rates. However, there is substantial evidence that by the 1970s many rail freight rates were not too high, but too low. The evidence supporting this view comes from several sources.

First, there were no controversial cases such as the Ingot Molds case, in which railroads were blocked from lowering rates because of barge competition.

Second, there were a number of cases in which the railroads applied for rate increases and the ICC either failed to grant them or granted them reluctantly. Indeed, the "market dominance" provision of the Railroad Revitalization and Regulatory Reform Act of 1976 (the 4R Act) gave the railroads what they took as license to raise rates freely on a wide variety of commodities, only to be frustrated in that goal by the ICC's interpretation of the act.

9. See John R. Meyer, Merton J. Peck, John Stenason, and Charles Zwick, *The Economics of Competition in the Transportation Industries* (Harvard University Press, 1959); Robert W. Harbeson, "Toward Better Resource Allocation in Transport," *Journal of Law and Economics*, vol. 12 (October 1969), pp. 321–38; and Ann F. Friedlaender, *The Dilemma of Freight Transport Regulation* (Brookings Institution, 1969), pp. 141–53.

10. See chapter 3, above.

Third, after the passage of the Staggers Rail Act of 1980, the most controversial changes sought by the railroads were large increases in rates on certain commodities. And for many commodities rail rates did increase after deregulation.

Fourth, the results of studies by academic economists changed dramatically. While they consistently argued in the 1950s and 1960s that rail rates, especially for manufactured commodities, should fall, in the 1970s similar studies argued that rail rates should rise, and in many cases rise quite substantially.

What normative benchmark should be used in evaluating rail regulation—that is, what should rail rates be in an efficient world? The traffic that flows only over routes for which economies of density have been exhausted can be priced at marginal costs, with all the benefits of competitive markets, provided, of course, that there is enough actual or potential competition (that is, contestability) to bring prices down to marginal costs. If, on the other hand, a shipment travels for at least part of its trip on a line operating below minimum efficient density, then marginal cost pricing will entail an operating loss that must be made up by government (or other) subsidies.

In a system where marginal cost is below average cost but in which subsidies are impossible, the welfare-maximizing solution is second-best, or Ramsey, pricing. This bears some resemblance to monopoly pricing in that price-cost margins under it are inversely proportional to demand elasticities. But Ramsey pricing allows price increases along these lines only up to the point at which a competitive return is earned, usually stopping short of the monopoly price (though the market for a service can be so weak that even a monopoly price cannot earn a competitive return).

There are thus two standards against which to compare existing rail rates: first-best marginal cost prices, and second-best Ramsey prices. But another benchmark is useful in the comparison: what the rates would actually be under deregulation, given the market structure and pricing policy of the railroad industry.

Three studies, all published in 1981, attempted to analyze these issues. Friedlaender and Spady analyzed what would happen to the markets for rail and truck transportation with marginal cost pricing for both modes; Levin examined marginal cost pricing, second-best pricing, and various plausible scenarios of monopoly and oligopoly pricing; and Winston examined the changes that would occur under marginal cost and Ramsey

Table 4-1. Friedlaender and Spady's Long-Run Equilibrium

Cents per ton-mile

Type of transportation and area	Actual rates		Rates based on long-run marginal costs	
	Manufactures	Bulk	Manufactures	Bulk
Rail				
Northeast	2.41	2.13	6.39	1.75
Rest of country	2.79	1.66	3.14	1.09
Truck				
Northeast	6.07	5.90	4.44	3.62
Rest of country	5.45	3.97	4.61	3.96

Source: Ann F. Friedlaender and Richard H. Spady, *Freight Transport Regulation: Equity, Efficiency, and Competition in the Rail and Trucking Industries* (MIT Press, 1981), pp. 143–61.

pricing.[11] None of these studies attempt to predict the outcome of deregulation; they are all conjectural exercises in determining what would happen if freight rates changed according to certain assumptions, which conceivably (though not necessarily) could occur under deregulation.

Friedlaender and Spady simulate the impact of marginal cost pricing for rail and trucking on rates, traffic carried, and profits for rail and truck transportation. Their simulations are based on statistically estimated cost functions (see chapter 3) and similarly estimated demand functions, which take account of the substitutability of rail and truck transportation (that is, a higher truck rate, when the rail rate is held constant, diverts some traffic to rail, and vice versa).

Table 4-1 summarizes Friedlaender and Spady's results on long-run competitive equilibrium in rail and truck transportation. Because of interregional differences in cost and demand functions, they separated their simulations for the Northeast from those of the rest of the country. They also did separate calculations for manufactured goods and bulk commodities. The table, based on their calculations, shows both actual rates and long-run marginal costs for rail and truck transportation.

The results indicate that, for trucking, all prices are above marginal costs and, for rail, rates are above marginal costs for bulk commodities

11. Ann F. Friedlaender and Richard H. Spady, *Freight Transport Regulation: Equity, Efficiency, and Competition in the Rail and Trucking Industries* (MIT Press, 1981), chap. 4; Richard C. Levin, "Railroad Rates, Profitability, and Welfare under Deregulation," *Bell Journal of Economics*, vol. 12 (Spring 1981), pp. 1–26; and Winston, "Welfare Effects of ICC Rate Regulation." Because the Winston study does not explicitly deal with the impact of ICC regulation on rates, it is discussed later in the chapter.

but below marginal costs for manufactures. Thus according to Friedlaender and Spady's predictions, rail rates on bulk commodities would fall by 18 percent in the Northeast with marginal cost pricing and by 35 percent in the rest of the country.[12] On the other hand, rates on manufactured goods would rise by 165 percent in the Northeast and by 14 percent elsewhere.

Friedlaender and Spady estimated that the net effect of these changes would be to increase railroad profits in the Northeast and reduce them elsewhere. They note that for the industry to earn a 9 percent return on investment (reasonably regarded as an opportunity cost of capital) long-run marginal cost pricing in the industry would have required an annual subsidy of $400 million as of 1972.

Based on their results, Friedlaender and Spady suggest that a long-run competitive equilibrium in freight transportation may be feasible and perhaps even likely under deregulation. This is because the relatively modest subsidy that long-run marginal cost pricing would require could probably be offset by the savings that abandoning a relatively small amount of low-density route-mileage could realize.[13] And they note that, if this was inadequate, rates could be increased somewhat above marginal costs on bulk commodities.

Nevertheless, Friedlaender and Spady qualify their results by saying that the competitive solution they propose might not be either technically or economically feasible. Certainly the potential need for subsidies can produce this problem. And in the carriage of bulk commodities, the railroads may well have enough market power so that marginal cost pricing, if it yielded enough revenues, would still be the result of regulation, rather than of competition. Finally, Friedlaender and Spady note that the sharp rate increases necessitated by a competitive solution, especially for manufactured goods in the Northeast, could place intolerably high burdens on northeastern shippers and manufacturers. Thus while they argue that marginal cost pricing for all commodities in the railroad industry is in principle feasible, they doubt that either real-world marketplaces or political considerations would actually allow it.

Friedlaender and Spady's calculations for a competitive equilibrium solution to the railroad problem are useful and illuminating, but their skepticism about the ultimate workability of marginal cost pricing in the

12. These percentages are calculated from table 4-1.
13. Friedlaender and Spady, *Freight Transport Regulation*, p. 162.

industry (in the absence of subsidies) is probably justified. In fact, they have probably given the competitive equilibrium solution the benefit of the doubt in evaluating it. This is true, first, because the specification of their long-run cost function overstates the percentage of costs that can be recovered through marginal cost pricing, especially on low-density routes; and second, because the very high rates that they find necessary to recover marginal costs for manufactured goods in the Northeast (over 60 percent above the truck rates, as shown in table 4-1) may not be feasible without diverting almost all traffic in these manufactures to trucks. For manufactured goods especially, the superior service provided by truck transportation is likely to make it the preferred mode when the rates charged for the two modes are the same. It is thus at least possible that Friedlaender and Spady's estimates of equilibrium rail and truck rates in the Northeast extrapolated a demand curve for rail services beyond the point at which all traffic would be diverted to truck transportation. Modifying their results to take account of these considerations would give even more reason to be skeptical about long-run marginal cost pricing (without subsidies) as a practical solution to the railroad problem. That is because marginal cost pricing would be less compensatory than they have estimated, and, particularly in the Northeast, the market might not support the degree of rate increases they conjecture. Nevertheless, their results do support one conclusion: on higher-density main-line rail routes, there is strong evidence of long-run constant returns to scale, and for many shipments flowing over these routes, long-run marginal cost pricing without subsidies is both feasible and desirable. If, however, such pricing is not always a feasible solution to the rail pricing problem, other pricing schemes should be considered.

Perhaps the most complete analysis of alternative pricing policies under deregulation is that of Levin.[14] He provides estimates of the likely changes in rates and railroad profitability resulting from four different sets of rail rates: marginal cost pricing, monopoly pricing, oligopoly (akin to Cournot) pricing, and Ramsey pricing. He also analyzes the effects of potential reductions in rail and truck costs under deregulation.

Some of Levin's results are shown in table 4-2. In essence, he finds the oligopoly results (which might correspond roughly to three-firm Cournot behavior) the most reasonable and plausible. On the one hand, he sees the ''cutthroat-competitive'' solution of marginal cost pricing as unrea-

14. "Railroad Rates."

Table 4-2. Rate Changes Resulting from Deregulation in the Levin Simulations
Percent

Type of commodity	Monopoly		3-firm interrailroad oligopoly	
	Old rate	New rate	Old rate	New rate
Bulk[a]				
Field crops	40.2	80.2	4.8	6.4
Produce	1.5	3.0	−34.0	−45.4
Iron ore	95.3	190.6	43.0	57.3
Coal	57.1	114.2	19.9	26.5
Manufactures	165	193	74.0	83.0

Source: Richard C. Levin, "Railroad Rates, Profitability, and Welfare under Deregulation," *Bell Journal of Economics*, vol. 12 (Spring 1981), pp. 15, 16.

a. Levin makes two calculations for bulk commodities, the first based on an econometric specification of a linear demand curve, and the second based on a specification of an exponential demand curve.

sonable in view of the mutually recognized independence of the small number of railroad firms. But he also argues that there are relatively few rail markets, especially for manufactured goods, where a single firm has a monopoly. While the number of "in-between" oligopoly solutions generates a fairly wide range of solutions, Levin nevertheless arrives at a plausible set of bounds for the rate increases likely under an oligopoly solution to the railroad problem in various U.S. markets, with average price increases ranging between 6 and 43 percent on manufactures and between 7 and 65 percent on bulk commodities. Levin calculates that these rate increases should generate returns on investment in the industry (on replacement value) of 4–8 percent after taxes, much better than the 1–2 percent realized in the years just before his study.[15]

Levin draws several other important conclusions from his results. First, the oligopoly prices he describes probably correspond roughly in their levels and welfare effects to Ramsey prices, although the lower-side returns on investment given are below an opportunity cost of capital.[16] Second, he calculates that an oligopolistic Ramsey solution to the railroad problem would mean a deadweight loss of roughly $1 billion a year in 1972 dollars but argues that it would be well worth such a loss to achieve the long-term viability of the industry.[17] Third, while he finds that the typical rate could rise under deregulation, he also finds that a

15. Ibid., p. 24.

16. That is, 4 percent on replacement value is probably inadequate. See chapter 1, above.

17. Levin, "Railroad Rates," p. 24.

significant percent (up to nearly 30 percent in the three-firm oligopoly model) would fall.[18]

Levin's analysis is entirely plausible, but it would be useful to know where within the range of rate increases the solution that rail markets would reach might fall. There is, of course, no way of answering this question with any certainty without waiting for rail deregulation to take its course for several years. But an additional and important piece of evidence can be brought to bear on this question.

In 1978 the staff of the Association of American Railroads calculated the likely costs of replacing rail transportation with truck transportation for all traffic in the United States now going by rail.[19] Any such calculations are likely to be crude, but the numbers from the AAR study suggest the extent to which rail rates can rise without diverting all traffic to truck (it is once again important to remember that for most commodities, if the rail rate is equal to or higher than the truck rate, the traffic will in all likelihood move by truck because of the superior quality of service offered by trucking). Also, these numbers on comparative rail and truck costs must be interpreted with caution because they are quite aggregate. They probably understate rail's advantage on high-density routes and overstate it on low-density routes. Finally, based as they are on gross truck weights of 80,000–90,000 pounds, they may understate truck costs on all but the heavier-duty highways, because some highways in the country are not built to withstand such heavy weights.

Despite all these qualifications, the results of the AAR study, shown in table 4-3, are illuminating. They indicate that for just about all commodities except coal, chemicals, minerals, and petroleum, rail enjoys a rather slim cost advantage over truck transportation. In all likelihood this explains why both the Friedlaender-Spady and Levin studies find that rail rates on manufactured commodities are so low relative to variable costs: truck competition places a tight constraint on the amount by which these rates can rise.

The evidence from the AAR study therefore provides a sharper view of the probable effects of rail deregulation on freight rates, especially for manufactured commodities, suggesting that rate increases, while they are certainly likely, will on the average be in the lower range suggested

18. This would occur with a 10 percent decline in both rail costs and truck rates, with deregulation in a three-firm competitive model. Ibid., p. 19.

19. Association of American Railroads Staff Studies Group, "The Economic Impact of Substituting Truck for Rail Transportation" (Washington, D.C.: AAR, July 5, 1978).

Table 4-3. Comparative Costs of Rail and Truck Transportation for Goods Now Carried by Rail

| Type of commodity | Estimated truck cost (cents per ton-mile) | | Actual rail cost (cents per mile) | 1977 rail ton-miles (billions) |
	80,000 pounds[a]	90,000 pounds[a]		
Farm products	3.0	2.7	2.7	8.2
Metallic minerals	4.3	3.9	5.2	17.0
Coal	4.3	3.9	2.2	182.0
Nonmetallic minerals	4.3	3.9	2.8	37.0
Lumber and wood	2.9	2.6	2.9	70.0
Pulp and paper	2.9	2.6	3.4	47.0
Chemical products	4.4	4.0	2.2	100.0
Petroleum products	4.4	4.0	3.0	29.0
Stone, clay, and glass	3.0	2.7	2.8	37.0
Primary metals	2.9	2.6	2.7	38.0
Transportation equipment	4.5	4.1	5.3	36.0
Waste and soap	3.0	2.7	9.8	6.0
Other	3.0	2.7	7.2	45.0

Source: Calculated from Association of American Railroads Staff Studies Group, "On the Economic Impact of Substituting Truck for Rail Transportation" (Washington, D.C.: AAR, July 5, 1978), p. 7.
a. Gross vehicle weight.

by these studies for most goods except chemicals: increases of 6 to 20 percent are more likely than increases of 60 percent or more.

For bulk commodities, on the other hand, these studies may understate the extent to which rate increases are feasible. Since 1972 (the year for which the Levin and Friedlaender-Spady studies were calibrated) the demand for shipping coal by rail has grown dramatically, and no facilities have been built for shipping it any other way. Since the opportunities for increased rail profits through rate increases in other commodities are limited, it would not be surprising if the railroads directed their efforts to increase rates at coal once regulatory ceilings are removed.

All the foregoing evidence suggests that deregulation should result, on the average, in modest rate increases for manufactured goods, and possibly more substantial rate increases for bulk commodities, with some reshuffling of rates within classes. But the studies cited so far are based on the aggregation of commodity types, whereas the discussion at the beginning of this chapter suggests that regulation has also caused distortions within commodity types between large and small shippers, high- and low-density routes, and so on.

Recent research by Boyer deals with this issue.[20] It indicates that,

20. Kenneth D. Boyer, "Equalizing Discrimination and Cartel Pricing in Transport Rate Regulation," *Journal of Political Economy*, vol. 89 (April 1981), pp. 270–86.

while average revenue yields for many rail commodity groups would not change with deregulation, rates on individual movements are likely to change dramatically in ways that could make both railroads and consumers better off. Specifically, working with a large sample of individual negotiated rail rates, Boyer finds that rates are apt to be based on a complicated combination of "fairness" rules; that is, they are set to ensure that one port or agricultural region has no advantage over another, that large shippers have no advantage over small ones, and so on. It seems that to protect the interests of some shippers and some regions, a significant amount of unprofitable traffic, somewhat akin to passenger traffic or low-density freight traffic in that it is uneconomic, is carried for reasons of equity.

Boyer finds a certain amount of "value-of-commodity" pricing in rail tariffs, wherein higher-value commodities go at higher price-cost margins. However, he argues that, with intermodal competition, higher-value commodities do not have lower freight demand elasticities, so that in fact the railroads are sacrificing profits from that pricing strategy.

Although Boyer finds substantial evidence of cross-subsidization of short hauls by long hauls, it is inconsistent with either monopoly pricing or Ramsey taxation. At the end of his detailed study, he concludes that "deregulating rail rates should not lead to a general increase or decrease in rail rates, but to a reshuffling of prices."[21]

Boyer's results generalize those of some earlier studies that dealt with rail rate structures for specific commodities and regions. A 1978 study by Horn found that rail rate equalization for ports had significant costs both to railroads and to consumers.[22] Similarly, in a 1979 study Hill showed that ICC policies blocking contract rates were costly to railroads and to the public.[23]

In a 1981 study Damus reported a detailed analysis of rail rates like that of Boyer but with an important difference: whereas Boyer worked with rates prevailing in the early 1970s, Damus used rail rates prevailing between 1870 and 1930.[24] But Damus's conclusions are strikingly similar to those of Boyer. He finds that, even before the ICC, rail rates on routes

21. Ibid., p. 282.
22. Kevin H. Horn, "Rail Rate Equalization to and from Ports: Some Preliminary Comments on Preliminary Content," *ICC Practitioners' Journal,* vol. 46 (November–December 1978), pp. 30–55.
23. Stephen G. Hill, "Contract Rates Increasing Rail Profitability," *ICC Practitioners' Journal,* vol. 46 (January–February 1979), pp. 222–32.
24. Sylvester Damus, "Two-Part Tariffs and Optimum Taxation: The Case of Railway Rates," *American Economic Review,* vol. 71 (March 1981), pp. 65–79.

with more than one firm were apt to be based on notions of equity or other such considerations. Because they were neither equal to marginal costs nor correlated with demand elasticities, they were inconsistent with competition, monopoly, or Ramsey prices. Like Boyer, Damus found that rail rates on competitive routes tended to cross-subsidize short hauls with profits from long hauls.

All the evidence presented here on regulated rail rates from the 1870s through the 1970s, then, points in one direction for theories of regulation. It supports the hypothesis of political-support maximization developed in the Chicago school and brought to its most general form by Peltzman. And just as predicted by Peltzman, the main beneficiaries are "disadvantaged" (high-cost) shippers, ports, agricultural regions, and the like. Although it may seem surprising that a "regulated" rail rate structure could predate the ICC, this is consistent with the evidence in chapter 2.

Regulation and System Size

Evidence presented previously on the regulatory behavior of state and federal agencies toward railroad abandonments indicates that regulatory policies have been geared to preserving a route system consistently larger than the marketplace as structured at present will support. This has been done through direct blockage of abandonments, offering the choice between subsidizing service at the federal or local level and seeing it abandoned, and a merger policy seemingly geared to avoid injury to weak railroads. But it is still possible that a system as large (or nearly as large) as the present one could be justified on a first-best benefit-cost basis. Several pieces of empirical evidence on this are available.

First, to test for the benefits of existing marginal low-density rail route-mileage, I have attempted to estimate an extremely simplified aggregate demand function for rail freight services. The idea behind this is simple: by estimating a time series aggregate demand function for rail services in the United States, subsuming all prices and tonnages into single indexes, it might be possible to get a crude measure of the extent to which route-mileage affects the aggregate demand for rail services and hence consumer benefits. If consumer benefits from route-mileage could be measured in this way, they could be compared with available estimates of the costs of extra route-mileage, giving some indication of how much the system is overextended.

Table 4-4. Regression Results of Estimated Demand for Rail Freight, 1947–78

Dependent variable: revenue ton-miles

Variable	Coefficient	t-statistic
Constant	8.465	2.96
Price	−1.588	−4.51
Route-miles	0.377	0.37
Real GNP	1.196	10.41
Miles of paved highways	−7.284	−9.29
Summary statistics		
$\bar{R}^2$ = 0.956		
Durbin-Watson = 2.002		

Sources: Railroad data from Interstate Commerce Commission, *Transport Statistics*, pt. 1, Second Release, 1947–78 (figures are for all Class I and Class II railroads); macroeconomic data from *Economic Report of the President, January 1980*, and Report of the Council of Economic Advisers, 1980; data on paved roads from Bureau of Public Roads, *Highway Statistics*, 1947–78.

The model estimated is as follows:

$$RTM = a_0 + a_1 P + a_2 MR + a_4 RGNP + a_5 PH,$$

where *RTM* is net revenue ton-miles of rail freight carried (in trillions), *P* is the price of rail services (in cents per ton-mile) converted to 1972 prices with the implicit GNP deflator (in a regulated market, that can more reasonably be treated as exogenous than in a competitive one), *MR* is route-miles of rail service, *RGNP* is real GNP in hundreds of billions of 1972 dollars, and *PH* is miles of paved highways in the United States as a proxy measure of the cost and quality of truck service available in a given year. The model was estimated over annual time series from 1947 through 1978. The results are shown in table 4-4. Despite the admitted crudeness of this procedure, all coefficients are of the right sign, and all but one are highly significant.

The coefficient that is both small and insignificant is the one for route-miles. It appears that in the range of abandonments that the railroads have applied for and the ICC has permitted, variations in route-mileage have not been sufficient to affect overall demand significantly. In other words, the effect of abandonments on net benefits, in the range in which they have occurred, is too small to pick up with the aggregative estimation procedure employed.

Independent evidence from other sources corroborates this result. In one survey Lang notes that rail abandonments have had a negligible effect on the economic well-being of a community.[25] Harris found that

25. A. Scheffer Lang, "The Great Economic Leveling-Out of the Intercity Freight

most low-density branch lines now operated by railroads (and until recently required by regulation) could not pass a benefit-cost test, even with the benefit of doubt given to continuation of service. [26]

All this suggests that, although there may be some benefits in preserving marginal miles of railroad, they are very small from the perspective of a benefit-cost analysis. That, in turn, provides strong evidence against the hypothesis of first-best optimizing behavior with respect to route-mileage. Although it is impossible to totally reject the model on this count, because conceivably it allows for greater route-mileage than does the first-best model, this evidence combined with evidence on pricing again supports the Peltzman model.

Indeed, the evidence on rates and on route capacity, taken together, suggests that regulatory policy on the two is conceptually equivalent. Service on low-density routes and on weak railroads can be viewed as equivalent to other services for which unprofitable rates are charged— short-haul service, service to small shippers, and service to disadvantaged ports. In each case, the railroad fulfills a common carrier obligation to offer unprofitable service at "just" rates to everyone. As long as there is enough high-profit service to support all these unprofitable ones, such a pattern is sustainable. As it ceases to be, regulatory reform should be expected to gradually ease up on the relevant common carrier obligations or to support them with general revenues.

Welfare Effects of Railroad Regulation

It is thus evident that public policies toward the railroad industry have generated something considerably different from a normative optimum of economic efficiency or even from a second-best policy. What have the welfare effects of rail regulatory policies been, and what is their value?

Studies along these lines have been pursued on and off for nearly twenty-five years, and the conclusions reached have varied. The only

Transportation Market," in Kenneth D. Boyer and William G. Shepherd, eds., *Economic Regulation: Essays in Honor of James R. Nelson* (Michigan State University Press, 1981), pp. 55–64.

26. Robert G. Harris, "Rationalizing the Railroad Freight Industry: A Case Study in Institutional Failure and Proposals for Reform," Sloan Working Paper 7705 (University of California at Berkeley, Department of Economics, September 1977).

thing to remain constant is the finding that ICC policies are inefficient. I classify the studies of losses from regulation into four categories: losses from minimum rates, losses from excess capacity, losses from maximum rates, and miscellaneous losses in productivity stemming from regulation of both rates and services. This is roughly consistent with the order in which these losses were studied over the years.

Rate Regulation

In the 1950s and 1960s minimum-rate regulation was believed to be the most important cause of welfare loss from ICC policies. Meyer and others in the late 1950s discovered that rail transportation was substantially cheaper than truck transportation for manufactured as well as for bulk commodities, especially for higher-value manufactured goods using piggyback (trailer-on-flatcar) service. Noting that much traffic currently went by truck that could more cheaply go by rail, Meyer and his associates argued that it was value-of-service pricing and the ICC minimum-rate regulation enforcing it that caused so much inefficient choice of transportation mode. According to this argument, if railroads were allowed to reduce rates freely, they would do so to the point where they would win much of the traffic currently being carried by truckers.[27]

Friedlaender went further than this, stating that in the absence of ICC regulation practically all traffic then going by truck would shift to rail.[28] Harbeson, making calculations similar to those of Friedlaender, argued that there was a welfare loss of $1.5 billion to $3 billion as a result of traffic being inefficiently carried by truck when it could be more efficiently carried by rail.[29]

These results were implicitly challenged by Peck,[30] who guessed that rail rate-making freedom would be more likely to expand rail revenues by only 10 percent than to more than double them, as they would have to do to win most truck traffic. And they were explicitly challenged by Hilton, who argued that rail transportation is subject to so much loss and damage and delay that it is an imperfect substitute for truck transportation, so that the rate reductions suggested by Meyer and

27. Meyer and others, *Economics of Competition.*
28. *The Dilemma of Freight Transport Regulation.*
29. "Toward Better Resource Allocation."
30. Merton J. Peck, "Competitive Policy for Transportation?" in Almarin Phillips, ed., *Perspectives on Antitrust Policy* (Princeton University Press, 1965), pp. 244–72.

others, Friedlaender, and Harbeson would win little truck traffic for rail.[31] All three of those studies took some account of the inferior quality of rail service, but they included only the inventory costs of slower line-haul travel times. They ignored yard delays resulting from the failure to connect cars to trains for which they were scheduled, as well as loss and damage costs.

This low cross-elasticity of demand between rail and truck transportation was in fact included in Friedlaender's 1969 estimated welfare loss from ICC regulation of $200 million to $300 million (in 1963 prices), rather than the $1.5 billion to $3 billion indicated by Harbeson.[32]

Subsequent work has confirmed that the real welfare loss from ICC rate regulation was much closer to $300 million than to $3 billion. The reason is that, as long as the rail rate is somewhat below the truck rate, the cross-elasticity between rail and truck transportation is likely to be low. To put it another way, since rail service is inferior to truck service, if the railroads raise their rates above truck rates, they will lose practically all traffic to trucks. If, on the other hand, railroads reduce their rates and truck rates remain constant, rail will win little extra traffic. This is supported by a substantial amount of research done in the 1970s.

In a 1977 study I analyzed the effects of deregulation on rail, truck, and water market shares in Australia, where interstate traffic has been deregulated for all modes of transportation since 1954.[33] The study presents strong evidence that Australian technology is similar to American technology and that relative factor price differences between the two countries should not affect the relative advantages of rail and truck transportation. I further pointed out that, as one would expect, price and service rivalry between rail and truck transportation has intensified as a result of deregulation, with railroads and forwarders adopting the latest and most sophisticated trailer-on-flatcar technologies to compete with trucks. Nevertheless, when controlled for length of haul, as of the

31. George W. Hilton, "The Costs to the Economy of the Interstate Commerce Commission," in a compendium of papers submitted to the Subcommittee on Priorities and Economy in Government of the Joint Economic Committee, *The Economics of Federal Subsidy Programs, Part 6—Transportation Studies*, 93 Cong. 1 sess. (Government Printing Office, 1973) pp. 707–33.

32. *The Dilemma of Freight Transport Regulation*, p. 74.

33. Theodore E. Keeler, "Regulation and Modal Market Shares in Long-Haul Freight Transport: A Statistical Comparison of Australia and the United States," in J. R. Nelson and H. O. Whitten, eds., *International Comparisons of Freight Regulatory Policies* (Washington, D.C.: Federal Railroad Administration, 1977), chap. 7.

early 1970s rail and truck market shares were almost exactly the same for equivalent manufactured commodities in Australia and the United States. This certainly supports the view that rate-making freedom would give U.S. railroads little opportunity to divert traffic in manufactures from trucks.

This is further supported by the work of Boyer and Levin.[34] Each of these researchers estimated discrete-choice demand functions for rail and truck transportation, and each estimated costs of ICC rate regulation (relative to marginal costs) of $100 million to $400 million (in 1969 dollars). In a 1976 paper reworking Friedlaender's 1969 results, I found a welfare loss of no more than $500 million (again in 1969 dollars).[35]

Based on the most sophisticated estimates of rail and truck demand functions yet (because of both better data and more advanced estimation techniques), Winston found a welfare loss (relative to marginal cost prices) somewhat higher than these estimates. He concluded that, as of the late 1960s, the welfare loss from rail regulation alone was roughly $750 million, although this was offset by the effects of truck regulation, which, because it raises the price of a substitute for rail transportation, reduces the welfare loss from rail rates above marginal costs.[36] With the offsetting effects of truck regulation, a welfare loss of no more than $500 million for the late 1960s, or roughly twice that for the late 1970s, is appropriate. Levin, acknowledging an earlier programming error, stated in 1981 that his estimates were consistent with Winston's.[37] Thus while the welfare loss from freight rate regulation is not as high as originally thought, it is nonetheless more than trivial, being in the late 1970s somewhere around $1 billion a year.

Boyer's 1981 study makes it seem quite possible that the welfare loss from freight regulation is even larger than the $1 billion suggested by Winston.[38] This is because all studies of the welfare effects of regulation have aggregated over commodity types. Yet Boyer's evidence suggests

34. Kenneth D. Boyer, "Minimum Rate Regulation, Modal Split Sensitivities, and the Railroad Problem," *Journal of Political Economy*, vol. 85 (June 1977), pp. 493–512; and Richard C. Levin, "Allocation in Surface Freight Transportation: Does Rate Regulation Matter?" *Bell Journal of Economics*, vol. 9 (Spring 1978), pp. 18–45.

35. Theodore E. Keeler, "On the Economic Impact of Railroad Freight Regulation," Sloan Working Paper 7601 (University of California at Berkeley, Department of Economics, September 1976).

36. Winston, "The Welfare Effects of ICC Rate Regulation Revisited."

37. "Railroad Rates," p. 23.

38. "Equalizing Discrimination."

that there are many rate distortions within commodity types that are impossible to quantify in any aggregative study of the effects of regulation. Price-cost margins that are lower for short hauls than for long hauls, rates that protect small shippers, and rates that protect ports and producing regions are all intracommodity distortions, and if the work of Boyer is correct, these distortions are likely to be important because eliminating them could have substantial effects on rail rates, profits, and shippers' welfare. Quantifying these benefits would be exceedingly difficult, given the level of disaggregation needed to calculate rate and welfare effects accurately.

One other point about the welfare effects of ICC regulation needs to be emphasized. All the results discussed so far compare the existing rate structure to the ideal of marginal cost pricing. Since most operations in the industry are currently subject to increasing returns to scale, this will of course not generate a financially viable industry. For that reason, Levin and Winston estimated the welfare effects of the second-best prices needed to make the industry financially viable (and Levin believes that realistic oligopoly prices in the industry would roughly approximate these Ramsey prices) and found that these prices would entail a considerable additional welfare loss ($1 billion or so a year), although they would make the industry self-sustaining. It has been argued in this chapter that these second-best prices are not feasible because, in general, they would drive rail rates above truck rates.

However, Boyer's 1981 results predict a happier world for railroads and consumers alike. They suggest that, without substantial increases in the rail rate level, railroads can still substantially increase their profits by restructuring their rates, emphasizing the services that are profitable to them, and letting less profitable traffic go to other modes. These changes, like route abandonments, will obviously be unattractive to some shippers, but both the public and the railroads should gain from them. Even if marginal cost pricing is neither feasible nor desirable, the restructuring suggested by Boyer could result in welfare improvements for consumers and better rail profits.

Excess Route-Mileage

Public regulation (state and ICC) has kept more miles of rail service in existence than a benefit-cost analysis can justify. How large are the losses from these policies? An upper bound of the costs of excess capacity can be estimated from the cost of carrying all existing traffic levels at minimum efficient traffic density. Since there could be no excess capacity induced by regulation if there were constant returns to traffic density, it would be impossible to save more than the difference between current costs and costs at minimum efficient density by abandoning excess capacity.

Using this method, Friedlaender found losses from excess capacity of roughly $2 billion as of the early 1960s.[39] Using different estimating methods, I found a loss of $1 billion to $3.5 billion as of the late 1960s.[40]

Clearly, the cost of excess route capacity in the industry is likely to be lower than this (I would guess that $1 billion might be more realistic). But without a complete benefit-cost analysis of the nation's rail system, it is impossible to tell for sure. Harris, however, considering only the lowest-density branch lines, found that as of 1977, if the railroads had eliminated all the unprofitable ones, they would have reaped one-time savings of $1.5 billion from property sales, $2 billion in deferred maintenance and rehabilitation costs, and annual operating costs of $140 million to $300 million.[41] With a 10 percent interest rate, this would correspond to annual savings of $500 million to $600 million or more. And Harris's analysis did not include many branch-line and main-line operations (still below minimum efficient density) that could have been consolidated effectively.

In his analysis of the potential benefits of branch-line abandonments, Harris surveyed the results of other studies of this issue and found most of them consistent with his own.[42] Furthermore, Friedlaender and Spady have since obtained results at least roughly consistent with those of Harris.[43]

Although some studies have found lower savings from rail abandonments than Harris did, they have arguably understated such savings. For example, they ignore the likelihood that most low-density lines, already in bad condition, will require some rehabilitation for continued

39. Ann F. Friedlaender, "The Social Costs of Regulating the Railroads," *American Economic Review*, vol. 61 (May 1971, *Papers and Proceedings, 1970*), p. 230.

40. "On the Economic Impact of Railroad Freight Regulation," p. 47.

41. Robert G. Harris, "Economic Analysis of Light Density Rail Lines," *Logistics and Transportation Review*, vol. 16 (January 1980), pp. 3–29.

42. Ibid.

43. *Freight Transport Regulation*, p. 200.

operation; or they build in labor constraints that may themselves be the result of public policies preventing abandonments.[44]

Based on all this evidence, a reasonable guess is that $500 million to $1 billion, or even more in 1977 prices, could be saved by eliminating excess route capacity. However, a considerable amount of route capacity has been or is being eliminated with the bankruptcy of the Rock Island and the Milwaukee, and other railroads are proposing to get rid of significant amounts of trackage too.

Freight Car Utilization

In addition to the inefficiencies caused by direct controls on railroad rates, there is evidence of considerable inefficiency caused by controls on rates (and rules) for freight cars. The controls affect both the rates one railroad pays for the use of another's cars off line and the rates shippers pay railroads for keeping cars at sidings. Two other aspects of freight rate regulation that also affect freight car utilization and operating efficiency are controls on the division of revenues for joint interline rates and common carrier notions of fairness prohibiting special rate discounts which could be used to fill cars that would otherwise return to their place of origin empty.

Rates paid by one railroad to another for off-line cars have two components: one varying with distance traveled on the given off-line railroad (mileage charge) and one varying with the time kept off line (per diem charge). Rates paid by a shipper for keeping a car on a siding (called "demurrage charges") are based on time kept. Regulation of these charges by the ICC has had distortive effects in each case.

Felton, among others, has argued that the ICC has generally kept the rates on cars for both per diem and mileage below the market-clearing price, thus forcing the railroads that own many cars (the "rich" railroads) to cross-subsidize the railroads that cannot afford many cars (the "poor" railroads).[45] Not surprisingly, this policy can be expected to have two effects. First, there should be a shortage of freight cars, at least under

---

44. For a summary of these studies and their conclusions, see "Rail Deregulation and Productivity" (Washington, D.C.: Public Interest Economics Center, July 1980), pp. 30–43.

45. John R. Felton, *The Economics of Freight Car Supply* (University of Nebraska Press, 1978).

some circumstances. Second, once a railroad had the car of another railroad, it would have little incentive to return the car to its home road. This would reduce its utilization rate. To counter this, the Association of American Railroads has set up rules requiring the prompt return of cars to their home roads, usually by the most direct route possible. But this rule, necessary if car hire rates are kept artificially low, is itself inefficient. If car rentals were properly set, the owning road would be very nearly indifferent whether the car was returned immediately or not, and if a loading was available by a more circuitous routing, the load would be carried with proper pricing. Thus the forced underpricing of freight cars not only created a shortage, but also made utilization inefficient, with more cars needed to haul a given amount of traffic than would have been necessary under a more market-oriented regime.

The distortions caused by regulated rates tended to force the use of other stopgap rules designed to overcome the workings of the market-place. The ICC often had to use common carrier obligation rules to force one railroad to make cars available to another at a below-market price. And during peak grain harvest periods, because peak-load pricing of cars was not allowed, there were perennial shortages of boxcars in regions where grain was being harvested. The ICC attempted to use nonmarket rules to correct these problems too.

It can be argued that the ICC held rates too high for car rentals overall, but there also appear to have been many specific circumstances in which rates were too high, especially for empty backhauls and off-peak periods. Cars were often returned to the home road too quickly when, with more time or greater distance traveled, the car could have been returned with a load.

Several studies have analyzed the cost to society of underutilization of the freight car fleet because of inappropriate per diem and mileage charges, including Barnakov, Felton, Sumner and Ferguson, and Ventura.[46] And a group of twelve railroads ran an experiment in the mid-1970s wherein they treated each other's cars as if they were their own

---

46. Christopher Barnakov, "The Potential Effects of Deregulation on Railroad Operating Costs" (Congressional Budget Office, 1980); Felton, *Economics of Freight Car Supply;* Jason Sumner and Allen Ferguson, "Deregulation and Fleet Efficiency" (Washington, D.C.: Public Interest Economics Center, July 1980); and Jack Sal Ventura, "Railroad Freight Cars: Economic Models of Investment and Allocation" (Ph.D. dissertation, Georgetown University, 1970).

Table 4-5. Estimated Costs of Inefficient Freight Car Utilization Caused by Regulation

Type of distortion	Cost (millions of dollars)
Inefficient mileage and per diem charges	
Capital costs	350
Operating costs	325
Inefficient demurrage charges (capital costs only)	560
Circuity from inefficient rate divisions	
Capital costs	137–225
Operating costs	128–256
Total savings	1,500–1,716

Source: Jason Sumner and Allen Ferguson, "Deregulation and Fleet Efficiency" (Washington, D.C.: Public Interest Economics Center, July 1980), pp. 64–65.

(that is, they attempted to use each car based on its true marginal costs, regardless of per diem and mileage costs).[47]

All the studies cited estimate similar orders of magnitude for the efficiency loss from freight car rental regulation. Sumner and Ferguson, in perhaps the most complete study, base their results on an analysis of the results of earlier studies and on substantial additional calculations. They find that efficient car hire pricing would generate an overall reduction in empty car-miles of 19 percent, for annual savings of $350 million in operating costs and $325 million in ownership costs, all in 1977 prices.[48] They note, furthermore, that more efficiency could be gained if these lower costs were passed on to shippers and consumers. According to Sumner and Ferguson, total welfare benefits from more efficient per diem and mileage rates should total at least $675 million. This amount is shown along with other regulatory effects on car fleet utilization efficiency in table 4-5.

Similarly, both the structure and level of demurrage rates create inefficiency in freight car use. In general, regulations covering these rates force the railroads to allow "free periods" during which the shipper need pay no more than the regular freight rate for keeping the car on the siding. Only after that time do demurrage rates start. If, upon payment of the full opportunity cost of the car, the shipper did not keep the car

47. A. D. Dingle, "Freight Car Clearinghouse Experiment—Evaluation of the Expanded Clearinghouse," AAR Report FR-292 (Association of American Railroads, January 15, 1978).

48. Sumner and Ferguson, "Deregulation," p. 64.

for the whole of the free period, this structural aspect of demurrage rates would cause underutilization of the car fleet. Many cases can be cited in which railroads have been forced to undercharge for demurrage, which encourages shippers to use freight cars as warehouses and wastes resources. This, like inadequate mileage and per diem rates, also tends to cause a shortage. Furthermore, if demurrage and per diem rates differ, market distortions will occur. A demurrage rate above a per diem rate will give a car-owning railroad an incentive to make cars available to shippers rather than to other railroads, and the opposite is true for a demurrage rate below a per diem rate.

Taking account of these complexities, Sumner and Ferguson estimate that the cost to society of car underutilization caused by inappropriate demurrage rates was $560 million as of 1977.[49] But they note that this number overstates the relevant welfare loss, because it does not count the benefits to shippers of being able to keep cars on sidings for inefficiently long times.

Freight rate regulation also indirectly affects car utilization and operating costs, for instance, revenue divisions of interline shipments among roads. Although the rate for the full interline shipment is set by the ICC, the division of rates between the two (or more) participating roads is determined by the relative mileages shipped on each connecting road. This gives the originating road an incentive to keep the shipment on its own road for as many miles as possible, even if this results in a highly circuitous routing overall. Originating railroads often practice "long-hauling" (shipping traffic over circuitous routing) to gain a favorable division of revenues.

It is difficult to estimate the overall cost of this practice, but Sumner and Ferguson note that the ICC, in setting rates in recent years, has generally assumed that the average shipment travels on a route 15 percent more circuitous than the shortest available rail route between any two points.[50] Some of this circuity is undoubtedly due to grades or curvatures on the short-line routes or to the physical difficulties or yard delays entailed in switching shipments to the shortest-line routes. Nevertheless, Sumner and Ferguson, as well as others studying this problem, have argued that a large part of the 15 percent circuity assumed by the ICC is due to distorted incentives from interline rate divisions.

49. Ibid., p. 65.
50. Ibid., pp. 42–43.

Depending on the portion of total circuity resulting from such distortions, Sumner and Ferguson estimate a total welfare loss of $260 million to $480 million a year as of 1977.[51] Once again, the efficiency gains from deregulation are likely to be greater to the extent that they are passed on in lower prices to shippers and consumers.

Finally, freight rate regulation has also reduced freight car utilization by failing to allow incentive or peak-load pricing to fill empty cars on backhauls while rationing the cars in peak directions and for peak periods. Estimates of these regulatory costs are not available, but they are probably substantial.[52]

Table 4-5 excludes these last costs in summarizing the costs of regulation. With the exception of the cost of demurrage, these costs are, if anything, conservative, but they are not small. They come to $1.5 billion to $1.7 billion, which is high relative to the costs of intermodal rate distortions or excess route-miles.

Rate Wars

It was argued above that the railroad industry is subject to increasing returns to scale on many of its routes and that, as a result, noncollusive pricing on the part of railroad firms would result in cutthroat competition, generating losses. As Levin has pointed out, with a sufficiently small number of firms, this is unlikely. For example, it is difficult to believe that the Canadian duopoly, even without the freedom to collude, would engage in extensive rate wars—recognition of mutual interdependence should prevent that. But as the number of firms increases, not only does coordination become more difficult, but also carriers' perceptions of the optimal price will differ, especially in the case of a weak competitor in need of additional business for survival.

On some routes, then, especially those with three or more competitors, rate wars could break out as a consequence of deregulation. Once it is granted, however, that the ICC has kept in existence more firms with more routes than are either commercially or socially desirable, it follows that rate wars would have a therapeutic effect on economic efficiency: they would persist until the weaker firms were driven out of business or at least forced to contract their services to routes with fewer firms. As

51. Ibid., pp. 64–65.
52. Ibid., pp. 59–62.

weaker firms went out of business, stronger ones would buy up routes with access to shippers that could be served profitably, and the number of carriers would shrink until the potential for rate wars had been eliminated. This does not mean that all service provided at increasing returns to traffic density would be eliminated (though it could and should be on many routes), but rather that the number of carriers would dwindle until coordination of rates above marginal costs became feasible, as suggested by Levin.[53]

In some regions of the United States, mergers have already reduced the number of firms providing service. Conrail already has a monopoly in the Northeast or shares a duopoly with one of several firms, among them the Norfolk and Western and the CSX. The South, on the other hand, generally has at most duopolies: the CSX and the Norfolk Southern. And with the bankruptcy of the Milwaukee, much of the Northwest has a Burlington Northern monopoly, but with considerable competition on some routes from the Union Pacific. On some major routes, such as Chicago–Los Angeles or Chicago–New Orleans, rate wars are still possible. But on most routes the number of rail rivals has already fallen so low that rate wars are unlikely. And if it is allowed to function, competition will reduce the number of carriers in other markets, eliminating the likelihood of rate wars there.

Evidence from Other Countries

Numerous countries around the world have to some degree deregulated rates, firm entry, and firm exit for freight transportation, including railroads.[54] Most, however, are not suitable for comparison with the United States. This is especially true of Western Europe, where hauls are much shorter than in the United States and the railroads concentrate on providing a combination of passenger and freight services very different from those provided by American railroads.

The experience of two countries, however, that have deregulated

---

53. "Railroad Rates."

54. For a compendium of evidence on freight regulatory policies in other countries, see J. R. Nelson and H. O. Whitten, eds., *Foreign Regulatory Experiments: Implications for the U.S.*, report prepared for the Department of Transportation (Annandale, Va.: H. O. Whitten Associates, 1977). See also Thomas Gale Moore, *Trucking Regulation: Lessons from Europe* (American Enterprise Institute for Public Policy Research, 1976).

freight, Australia and Canada, is relevant to the United States. Both countries are similar to this nation in factor prices, technologies used, length of haul, and other relevant socioeconomic dimensions, and market deregulation has been around long enough in both to indicate long-run effects. In Australia interstate freight transport was deregulated in 1954, based on a court interpretation of a constitutional provision that commerce among the Australian states was to be absolutely free. Freight transport on some Australian intrastate routes has been deregulated by legislative means since 1968. In Canada railroads have substantial rate-making freedom (including the freedom to collude on rates for competing routes) acquired through legislative reforms of 1967. In Canada, however, unlike Australia, interstate (and some intrastate) truck transportation is still regulated, with rates controlled and entry of new firms blocked.

Evidence from Canada seems more directly relevant to the United States, given the physical proximity of Canada and the greater similarities in technologies. On the other hand, Australia provides evidence not available from Canada on the impact of complete truck deregulation on markets for long-haul freight transport.

In Canada there have been few problems either with rates that shippers consider excessively high or with destructive competition.[55] Canadian shippers are protected by a ceiling, 160 percent of variable costs, deemed to constitute maximum reasonable rates. Between 1967 and 1980 only one shipper complained that rates were unreasonably high. (However, Canada's most important bulk commodity, grain, is protected by a rate ceiling that the railroads and most others studying rates would say is kept far too low.) In general, then, with the exception of grain, there is no evidence from Canada that maximum-rate regulation is needed to achieve rates acceptable to shippers. It is perhaps not surprising, with a nationwide rail duopoly which is free to collude on rates, that rate wars are not a problem in Canada.

What effect, if any, has deregulation had on Canadian rail rates,

---

55. A substantial amount of research has been done on freight deregulation in Canada. For general discussions of institutions and overall evidence, see T. Heaver and J. Nelson, *Railway Pricing under Commercial Freedom: The Canadian Experience* (Vancouver: University of British Columbia, Center for Transportation Studies, 1977); James Baldwin, "The Canadian Experience: Increased Rail Rate Freedom and Increased Subsidization as Successors to Rail Cross-Subsidization," in Nelson and Whitten, *Foreign Regulatory Experiments,* chap. 2; and T. Heaver, "Railroad Deregulation in Canada and Its Applicability to the U.S." (Washington, D.C.: Public Interest Economics Center, 1980).

service, and profitability? Its most important effect seems to have been on the structure of rates. There is far more reliance on contract and incentive rates in Canada than there was under the pre-1967 regulatory regime.[56] The aim of these rates is to use rail plant and equipment more effectively, which is generally achievable with large, regular shipments, or to fill backhauls of equipment that is empty during an off-season period. Incentive rates are likely to pass some of the savings from such operations on to shippers and keep some for the railroads.

The most detailed studies of rail deregulation in Canada have been done by Caves and Christensen.[57] Comparing levels of various measures of output per unit of input, they found that, although the Canadian railroads started out at lower productivity levels than U.S. carriers before 1967, the productivity of Canadian roads grew much faster between 1967 and 1977 and had reached a higher absolute level than that achieved by the U.S. carriers at the end of the period. Caves and Christensen argue that because nearly everything else between the two countries was constant, the relative success of the Canadian carriers must be due to differences in regulatory policy. They also argue that had U.S. railroads not been regulated as of 1974, higher productivity could have reduced their costs by as much as $6.7 billion a year.

How much freight deregulation has benefited the Canadian railroads in terms of profits is not so clear. While evidence needed for a direct comparison of the sort presented in chapter 3 is not available, considerable evidence does exist that for most of the 1970s the Canadian railroads fell considerably short of earning an opportunity cost of capital, making them much like their U.S. counterparts in that respect.[58] On the other hand, the fact that Canadian National (formed earlier from a group of insolvent private railroads) now earns a respectable return compared with private U.S. railroads may in itself be a sign of the positive effects of deregulation.[59]

One other area in which Canadian deregulation appears to have had some impact is in multimodal organization of transportation firms.

56. Heaver, "Railroad Deregulation," p. 25.

57. Douglas W. Caves and Laurits R. Christensen, "The High Cost of Regulating U.S. Railroads," *Regulation*, vol. 5 (January–February 1981), pp. 41–46.

58. Canadian Pacific Rail's return on investment ranged between 3.0 percent in the 1960s and 7.4 percent in 1977. See Heaver, "Railroad Deregulation," p. 28.

59. In 1980 the Canadian National earned a return on book value of roughly 10 percent, putting it on a level with some relatively prosperous U.S. railroads. Frank Malone, "Marketing-Minded CN Looks West," *Railway Age*, vol. 182 (May 25, 1981), pp. 48–77.

Friedlaender and Harrington found that a larger part of rail shipments of manufactured goods go by piggyback in Canada than in the United States.[60] They attribute this to the fact that until 1980 the piggyback service of American railroads was tightly controlled both in rates and in the distance from the rail terminal that piggyback shipments could be carried over the highway. Friedlaender and Harrington also found, however, that as of 1974 the market share of rail for all shipments that could go by piggyback in Canada was actually smaller than the equivalent rail market share in the United States. (The market share of tons of containerizable freight shipped by rail in the United States was 58.7 percent, versus 51.0 percent in Canada.)[61] Thus while more intermodally oriented transportation companies encourage the use of trailer-on-flatcar, this seems to add relatively little to rail's ability to win a larger market share from truck.

The evidence from both Australia and Canada on the deregulation of intermodal freight is quite useful.[62] Because Australia has had complete truck deregulation for many years, intermodal transportation companies have reached an even higher level of development there than in Canada. Specifically, not only do Australian railroads provide extensive multimodal services, but also, since there are no entry barriers in trucking, a new type of highly competitive industry has developed: multimodal forwarder truckers. In essence, these are trucking firms that also operate piggyback yards and charter entire trains at contract rates between major Australian cities. More than in Canada, the Australian interstate markets suggest what complete freight deregulation can accomplish in the way of efficiency. First, empty backhauls are rare.[63] Second, there is plenty of evidence that the pricing and service levels of these forwarder truckers are the product of highly competitive markets for both truck and intermodal transport. This comes both from direct observation of price-cost margins[64] and

60. Ann F. Friedlaender and Ian Harrington, "Intermodalism and Integrated Transport Companies in the United States and Canada," *Journal of Transport Economics and Policy*, vol. 12 (September 1979), pp. 247–55.

61. Ibid., p. 262.

62. The seminal work on Australian freight deregulation is Stewart Joy, "Unregulated Road Haulage: The Australian Experience," *Oxford Economic Papers*, vol. 16 (July 1964), pp. 274–85. Many other pieces have been written in this area, most of which are summarized in my "Regulation and Modal Market Shares," chap. 9. See also Peter J. Rimmer, *Freight Forwarding in Australia* (Canberra: Australian National University, 1970).

63. Joy, "Unregulated Road Haulage," pp. 278–80.

64. Ibid.

from evidence on the profitability of the carriers. The manager of terminal facilities for one such firm (who preferred not to be identified) said that management of the conglomerate that owned his firm had on several occasions considered selling it because of inadequate profits. After close examination in each case, however, the conglomerate decided to keep the firm because the return was just sufficient to make it worthwhile. That, of course, is the textbook definition of a competitive market.

The Australian form of free market organization is also attractive because it helps ensure that small shippers are not the objects of true economic discrimination. That is, the forwarders appear to have passed on all the benefits of contract rates and large-volume shipping that they have managed to obtain from the railroads.

Although the Australian form of organization has achieved a relatively high level of efficiency and productivity through intermodal operations, it is less clear that it has also achieved for the railroads (owned by the states or in some cases by the commonwealth government) either higher levels of profitability or a larger market share. It has in fact been documented that in Australia the market share of rail transportation in manufactured goods over a given distance is no higher than for equivalent markets in the United States. This evidence for Australia is consistent with Friedlaender and Harrington's evidence for Canada. As for profitability, while the forwarders appear to earn an adequate return, the railroads claim to earn no more than variable costs on their intermodal interstate traffic. Thus the evidence on intermodal traffic from both Australia and Canada suggests that it can be operated with considerably greater productivity under deregulation and that it can benefit small shippers by ensuring that any truly discriminatory prices are arbitraged away by the forces of market competition. On the other hand, it is less clear that deregulation would allow rail piggyback transport to divert a larger market share from trucking, especially if rates charged and services provided are profitable.

Overall, though, it is probably safe to conclude on the basis of evidence from abroad that freight deregulation will enhance the well-being of both consumers and rail investors by allowing the carriers to pursue only business that is profitable and to tailor their rates and services to make the most efficient possible use of their equipment. That is certainly consistent with the evidence from studies of the potential effects of deregulation in the United States.

An Overview

Although rate regulation, car-hire regulation, and abandonment have been discussed separately, it should be evident by now that the distinction among them is conceptually an artificial one. The underlying principle is the same, and it goes back to the medieval principle of common carriage. According to that principle, fairness demands that high-cost users be served, and served on terms less favorable to the carriers than serving low-cost users. Railroads have been obliged to service small shippers, low-density routes, short-haul users, disadvantaged ports and agricultural regions, shippers located on financially weak railroads, and, at one time, passengers, all at less-than-compensatory prices and to the disadvantage of themselves and their more economic users. For railroads, deregulation of rates and of service obligations go hand in hand; such deregulation would allow the industry either to price each service at a compensatory level or to eliminate it. The potential savings from route abandonments alone are probably but a small fraction of the savings affordable from revoking all common carrier service obligations.

It is therefore likely that relief from these obligations in both rates and services could in some cases generate improved profits for railroads and lower prices for consumers. Flexibility in rates charged and services provided will probably increase the productivity of railroads considerably through better utilization and rationalization of both plant and equipment. The dollar value of the potential benefits from this deregulation is impossible to estimate, but it would probably have been well over $1 billion a year in the late 1970s, just before passage of the Staggers Rail Act.

The main losers from rail deregulation would be those receiving money-losing services. For a number of them, such as small shippers, short-haul users, and those on low-density lines, truck service should provide an economic substitute. As the aggregative evidence presented in table 4-3 indicates, rail's cost advantage over truck is very small for most commodities except coal, chemicals, and minerals, and for the type of shipments for which rail is least economic, truck probably has a real cost advantage over rail. Doing away with the services for which rail is uneconomic will by definition leave it with the traffic that gives it a clear advantage. The development of the interstate highway system has made any notion of common carrier service obligations for railroads obsolete.

CHAPTER FIVE

Regulatory Reform
and Its Consequences

IN THE LATE 1970s pressure mounted for further deregulation of the railroad industry. There were several reasons for this.

First, the provisions of the Railroad Revitalization and Regulatory Reform Act of 1976 that allowed some rate-making freedom were largely emasculated by Interstate Commerce Commission interpretations—just about everywhere the railroads had the discretionary power to raise rates in accordance with the act, the ICC found the existence of market dominance. So the railroads urged further freedom. And in many areas, such as contract rates, the 4R Act held out little hope for reform anyway.

Second, the financial state of the carriers deteriorated: Conrail lost considerable money, and the Milwaukee and Rock Island Railroads went bankrupt. Moreover, the studies of rail viability by the Federal Railroad Administration (mandated by the 4R Act) indicated that the financial situation would worsen as time went on, requiring further reform.[1]

Third, there was a growing body of evidence that regulation, not only of railroads but also of airlines, was causing great inefficiencies and that more reliance on market forces could generate better service to shippers and travelers at lower prices.[2] To many observers, deregulation of domestic air transportation in 1978 was highly successful in producing lower fares and better service, and both the Carter administration and influential members of Congress hoped to duplicate this success in surface transportation.[3]

1. For a summary of the results of these studies, see Brock Adams, *A Prospectus for Change in the Railroad Freight Industry* (U.S. Department of Transportation, 1979).

2. For a summary of evidence on airline regulation, see Theodore E. Keeler, "The Revolution in Airline Regulation," in Leonard W. Weiss and Michael W. Klass, eds., *Case Studies in Regulation: Revolution and Reform* (Little, Brown, 1981), pp. 53–85.

3. Ibid., pp. 69–83.

Following up on work that had been started by the Ford administration, the Carter administration set about working with Congress to draft bills for rail and truck deregulation in 1978. (ICC chairman Daniel O'Neill had begun the process of regulatory reform in the commission in 1977 and 1978.) To speed up the process, in 1979 the Carter administration appointed to the ICC two pro-deregulation economists, Darius Gaskins (chairman) and Marcus Alexis. Gaskins and Alexis started by removing railroad rates on fresh produce from ICC control on the grounds that the railroads had a very small market share of this commodity, and hence no meaningful market power.[4] Based on existing laws, the ICC also attempted to decontrol rates in other areas, and for the first time explicitly allowed rail rates that would bring a return on investment. They encouraged railroads to apply for abandonments under the relatively liberal provisions of the 4R Act.

Despite the progress that was made, however, it was widely agreed that if rail deregulation was to succeed new legislation would have to be passed. Without it, the potential for legal challenges to any major changes was considerable.

Perhaps the greatest roadblocks to rail deregulation, under existing law and new legislation, were cities and public utilities, which feared large increases in rail coal rates.[5] On one hand, the railroads felt that freedom to raise rates on coal was an important part of any deregulation package; on the other, interests representing public utilities and consumers strongly opposed increases. Nevertheless, a compromise was reached.

The Staggers Rail Act of 1980

After much debate, the Staggers Rail Act was passed by both houses of Congress and signed by President Carter on October 14, 1980.[6] This

---

4. A brief discussion of these effects may be found in Kenneth D. Boyer, "Equalizing Discrimination and Cartel Pricing in Transport Rate Regulation," *Journal of Political Economy*, vol. 89 (April 1981), p. 282. See also Boyer's references.

5. The most notorious case of this was for coal shipped on the Burlington Northern between the Powder River Basin in Wyoming and certain cities in Texas. The Burlington Northern had originally quoted much lower rates to certain public utilities than it subsequently said it had to charge to break even on the traffic. See, for example, Paul Gibson, "A Railroad for the Long Haul," *Forbes* (April 27, 1981), pp. 120–26.

6. Public Law 96-448.

law was the most dramatic change in federal policy toward the railroads since the Interstate Commerce Act of 1887—in some ways an even more dramatic change than that law, because while the 1887 act codified principles already existing in common law (as applied to common carriers), the Staggers Act completely reversed earlier policies. It overturned not only many principles developed directly from the 1887 act, but also many principles of common carriage predating 1887. Obviously, the Staggers Act is important and worth considering in some detail.

The act is based on the premise (stated in section 2) that while the railroad industry once constituted a monopoly, requiring ICC regulation, this is no longer so. Most transportation is competitive and much ICC regulation has had an adverse effect on economic efficiency, as well as forcing the railroad industry to accept a return on investment far below the level adequate to maintain financial viability and finance future growth. The act assumes that less regulation and more reliance on the marketplace will help assure a better rail system and more efficient use of it, which should save energy and reduce inflation.

The act's goals (section 3) include assisting the industry in its rehabilitation under private ownership; reforming federal regulatory policy to achieve an efficient, economical, and stable system; and providing the regulation necessary to balance the needs of carriers, shippers, and the public.

The way the act intends to attain these goals is simple in principle: it aims to reduce common carrier obligations to provide either unprofitable services or profitable services at unprofitable prices. To put it another way, it sharply reduces the carriers' obligations to cross-subsidize money-losing services, allowing them instead to restructure rates and services to realize a profit or to discontinue the services if that is impossible. Regulation is preserved only to prevent prices from rising to monopoly levels for commodities of captive shippers and to prevent rates from falling to truly cutthroat levels. Although the principles are simple, the ways in which the act proposes to implement them legally are more complicated.

Rates

Possibly the most fought-over provision of the Staggers Act was that pertaining to maximum rates (sections 201 to 203). In the final version, the act amended the 4R Act to state that, except where a railroad had "market dominance," it would be free to set rates as it chose. Since the ICC had found that in almost every case in which the industry had the discretionary power to raise rates, it had market dominance, this change alone might have had little impact on the railroads' ability to raise rates. So another provision was added. It stipulated that, in addition to the 4R provisions, a carrier does not have market dominance if the ratio of revenues to variable costs for a given commodity is not above a specific ratio. This ratio started at 160 percent in 1980 and was to rise to between 170 and 180 percent in 1985 by increments of 5 percentage points a year (section 202). Just what maximum rate a carrier would be allowed to charge after 1984 was to be determined by how close it was to earning an "adequate" return on investment. Specifically, the maximum allowable ratio of revenue to variable cost would be determined by cutting off the distribution of revenue-to-variable-cost ratios at the lowest ratio consistent with an adequate return. In essence, then, the Staggers Act attempts to spread evenly among all captive shippers the burden of covering fixed costs, subject to the stipulation that railroads may charge at least 170 percent of the variable costs (but no more than 180 percent) for any commodity. The act also allows a carrier to raise rates under two other provisions. First, carriers not deemed to be earning an adequate return are allowed a zone of rate flexibility around existing "base" rates, which could, depending on the current level of rates, allow the carrier to raise rates to as much as 190 percent of variable costs (section 203). Second, the act stipulates that to account for inflation the ICC must specify a railroad cost index as a basis for automatic quarterly rate increases (section 206).

The act also sets a rate floor (section 201[c]). The floor, however, is clearly stated to be variable costs, the floor that the railroad industry itself argued was the appropriate one through the minimum-rate regulation cases of the 1950s and 1960s.

Furthermore, the Staggers Act gives the commission the option of exempting rail transport of certain commodity groups from regulation altogether. This is permitted when intermodal competition is so strong that regulation is unnecessary to assure economical prices and represents a legal sanction of what the ICC had already done for fresh fruits and vegetables.

At least as important as the ceilings and floors set for rail rates by the Staggers Act are its provisions relating to rate structure. Reversing not only ICC policy but also the common law that preceded it, it permits contract rates on a much greater scale than previously. Specifically, contracts are generally allowed provided that their terms are published and on file with the ICC for all to see (section 208). Contract rates can be opposed by shippers and ports if they can show that such rates represent unfair discrimination. (Competing carriers, however, are forbidden to oppose contract rates.) The act provides for flexibility in car-hire rates to encourage better utilization of the car fleet (section 224).

Besides allowing more flexibility in single-line rates, the act allows one carrier that is not receiving adequate revenues from joint rates to unilaterally add a surcharge (section 217).

Although the act grants increased flexibility in rail rates, it reduces freedom to collude in setting rates. It phases out the right, contained in the Reed-Bullwinkle Act of 1948, of railroads to collude through rate bureaus and it allows collective rate making only for carriers setting joint interline rates (section 219). Only carriers that are actually providing the transportation are allowed to participate in negotiating a given rate. The reason for this is obvious—if competition is to be the main vehicle for achieving efficient rates, it must be allowed to occur.

Abandonments and Mergers

The 4R Act had already liberalized the provisions for rail abandon-ments; the Staggers Act liberalizes them further in two ways. First, it sets a time limit on the length of the abandonment proceedings: it requires that the entire decision process be completed within 255 days of the date of application, including response to appeals (section 402). This is an important liberalization, because one of the strongest past deterrents to abandonments was the long, costly legal proceeding facing a railroad wishing to make them. Second, because the Staggers Act indicates clearly that a railroad's costs should include an opportunity cost of capital as a return on investment, it is much easier to demonstrate that an abandonment is justified, based on meaningful economic criteria (using only a cash-flow definition of costs, as the ICC had previously done, forced the railroad to provide services failing to earn an opportunity cost of capital).[7] Moreover, to make it easier to relieve the railroad of the burden of money-losing service deemed socially necessary by a local

7. The need for a compensatory return on investment is expressed in section 101, paragraph 10101a(6), and in the preceding discussion of rates.

government or shipping group, the act sets up a procedure for subsidy or transfer to another operator of these services. The act specifies that subsidies must include a return on investment (section 402).

The Staggers Act also facilitates mergers by accelerating the proceedings, broadening to all railroads the requirement that a decision be forthcoming within 300 days of the initial application (section 228). This is obviously designed to prevent such occurrences as the Union Pacific–Rock Island merger, which was considered for ten years and never decided.

Other provisions of the Staggers Act relate to federal assistance for unprofitable branch-line operations (all of title IV), improved rail cost estimation for ICC rate proceedings (title III), and labor protection for Conrail (title V). Only the last of these three sets of provisions could be said to be inefficient economically—it guarantees lifetime employment to all Conrail employees holding a position as of September 1, 1979.

Overall, then, the Staggers Act gives belated recognition to the fact that the railroad industry is no longer the monopoly it was in the nineteenth century and no longer able to cross-subsidize common carrier obligations of all sorts from profits on captive shippers. In fact, in recognizing that cross-subsidies come at the expense of captive shippers and in placing limits on prices they can be charged, the act actually discourages cross-subsidization and explicitly encourages raising rates or terminating money-losing services.[8]

Implications of the Act

Although the Staggers Act represents the sharpest shift in federal regulatory law covering rail transportation since the Interstate Commerce Act of 1887, it contains many provisions so ambiguous that it will take some time to determine their meaning in practice. For example, as this was written, no lawyers, either with railroads or in the Justice Department, knew just which collective rate-making activities were legal and which ones were not.[9] And the ICC still had to determine what constituted reasonable rates under different circumstances. Yet by 1982 some clear changes had emerged. Rates and services had certainly

8. Paragraph 10101a(10) specifically states that a part of national rail policy will be "the elimination of noncompensatory rates for rail transportation."

9. Robert C. Dart, "Caution Marks Railroad Rate Setting as Industry Studies Antitrust Issues," *Traffic World*, vol. 185 (February 2, 1981), p. 16.

become more flexible. Abandonments had increased, and the need to cross-subsidize common carrier obligations had fallen.

This is the most recent change in a long line of regulatory evolution that started with the Transportation Act of 1920, which liberalized abandonments by taking them out of the hands of state agencies and placing them under the control of the ICC. Although the Motor Carrier Act of 1935 and the Transportation Act of 1940 both attempted to increase the degree of cross-subsidization (or preserve that already existing), the Transportation Act of 1958 continued the trend toward relaxing rail common carrier obligations. It shifted discontinuance of passenger train service from state to ICC control, as the Transportation Act of 1920 had done for freight service. It slightly increased rail rate-making freedom by moving away from the notion that cartelized rates in some markets should be used to cross-subsidize service in other markets.

The National Rail Passenger Act of 1971 and the Regional Rail Reorganization Act of 1973 continued this process. Both provided substantial direct subsidies for money-losing services, freeing privately owned railroads from cross-subsidizing common carrier obligations for which they no longer had the necessary profits.

The 4R Act of 1976 continued the same pattern of relief from common carrier obligations. It liberalized abandonment criteria, increased rate flexibility, and provided for further government subsidy of lines that were not commercially viable and that railroads might want to abandon.

The Staggers Act, although it made much greater changes than the preceding acts, is nevertheless quite consistent with the trends in regulation that led up to it. It achieves liberalization of common carrier obligations by its provisions covering not only rates and abandonments but also mergers. The ICC's policies on mergers were seemingly motivated by a desire to preserve service on money-losing routes as much as by a desire to preserve competition (and help weak competitors) in any economic sense. Easing the common carrier obligation to retain money-losing service eliminated an important reason for blocking mergers.

Rail Deregulation

Regulatory reform in the railroad industry really came with the appointment by President Carter in 1979 of commissioners who favored deregulation. Using the available statutory provisions of the 4R Act, they not only deregulated fresh produce in advance of the Staggers Act reforms, but also introduced policies that could eventually improve rail financial viability.

The commissioners' first strong impact on abandonments was felt with the bankruptcies of the Milwaukee and Rock Island Railroads. Rather than try to force the bankrupt carriers to continue service, the ICC strongly encouraged the liquidation of the Rock Island and drastically reduced system size for the Milwaukee. In fact, the commission was reluctant to allow the Milwaukee to continue to operate, even though its management wanted to do so, under conditions that the commission did not believe to be financially sustainable.[10]

Similarly, the commission started granting contract rates well before the Staggers Act was passed, and by the end of 1980 many railroads had negotiated new contract rate agreements. Although contract rates still accounted for a relatively small percentage of rail freight shipped in 1980 and 1981, they were rapidly growing in popularity and promised to become an important tool for railroad pricing, as they had under deregulation in Australia and Canada.[11]

The commission approved four of the largest mergers ever. One combined the Burlington Northern and the Frisco; another combined the Chesapeake and Ohio and its affiliated roads with the Family Lines, a group of railroads that included the Louisville and Nashville and the Seaboard Coast Line;[12] a third combined the Norfolk and Western and the Southern; and the fourth combined the Union Pacific with the Missouri Pacific and the Western Pacific.

The activity of the commission on rate deregulation accelerated with the passage of the Staggers Act. Despite the vehement objection of some shippers, the commission set the maximum allowable return on investment at 11.7 percent after taxes, as of the spring of 1981, with adjustments to be made from time to time to account for changes in interest rates.[13]

10. Interstate Commerce Commission Staff, *The Prospect for Reorganizing the Milwaukee Road as a Viable Carrier* (Washington, D.C.: ICC, 1980).

11. See, for example, Robert C. Dart, "Rail-Shipper Contract Marketing Idea: Still on Launching Pad After Three Years," *Traffic World,* vol. 185 (March 2, 1981), p. 12. Some sense of the progress made one year later can be found in Frank Malone, "Contract Rates Are Catching On," *Railway Age,* vol. 183 (February 22, 1982), pp. 42–44.

12. A description of this merger may be found in Gibson, "A Railroad for the Long Haul," pp. 120–26. A description of the CSX merger may be found in T. Kizzia, "Chessie-SCL Industries: A Merger of Equals," *Railway Age,* vol. 182 (March 30, 1981), pp. 26–30.

13. Interstate Commerce Commission, *Ex parte* 193, decided March 26, 1981.

The commission's policies on rates became even more permissive than before, and in the spring of 1981 it exempted all trailer-on-flatcar movements from regulation of any sort.[14]

In mid-1981 the commission liberalized its criteria for rail market dominance, making it easier to exempt railroads from all controls.[15] Specifically, the new guidelines took the presence of intrarail, intermodal, or even interlocational competition as reason to exempt.

From an economic point of view, these changes all made good sense, since there is considerable evidence that, with the exception of bulk commodities usually shipped in hopper cars and chemicals usually shipped in tank cars, railroads generally do not have substantial cost advantages over trucking. There is thus little reason to regulate rates.

ICC policies on abandonments have become far more permissive since 1979. Table 5-1 shows the number of miles involved in abandonments applied for and granted by the ICC from 1946 through 1981. Although the number applied for and granted rose sharply over the period, this still understates the degree to which the ICC has liberalized rail abandonments. Table 5-2 shows, for 1979–81 and the first two months of 1982, the number of miles involved in abandonments granted, denied, and withdrawn. The withdrawals indicate instances where state, local, or shipper support was found for the line, relieving the railroad of some of its burden. In general, this did not occur before the mid-1970s, so abandonment applications not approved (table 5-1) were simply denied.

But for 1979, 1980, and 1981 it should be evident from table 5-2 that abandonments denied were reduced to practically nothing. There were still some denials, but the number was small compared with abandonments applied for, which were up sharply from earlier years.

All these legal changes have substantially reduced the common carrier obligations of the railroad industry, moving in an economically appropriate direction.

Economic Effects of Deregulation

Since even the legal meaning of the Staggers Act is not yet established, it is beyond the scope of this study to provide anything like a full

14. "ICC Adopts Rules Exempting Railroad Piggyback Service from Regulation," *Traffic World*, vol. 185 (March 2, 1981), p. 50.

15. *Railway Age*, vol. 182 (July 27, 1981), p. 16.

Table 5-1. Number of Miles Requested and Granted in Railroad Abandonments Applied for, 1946–78

Year	Miles requested	Miles granted
1946	1,747	670
1947	1,074	1,241
1948	781	907
1949	1,178	1,185
1950	886	955
1951	815	564
1952	1,294	1,306
1953	976	1,102
1954	498	873
1955	975	514
1956	731	822
1957	1,190	589
1958	2,062	1,825
1959	1,203	1,180
1960	1,602	772
1961	1,140	1,167
1962	1,616	1,582
1963	1,937	1,688
1964	1,528	811
1965	2,224	1,538
1966	1,920	1,054
1967	860	817
1968	2,036	1,890
1969	2,287	1,320
1970	1,762	1,782
1971	3,142	1,287
1972	3,978	3,458
1973	4,436	2,428
1974	2,247	529
1975	3,308	708
1976	1,634	1,788
1977	n.a.	2,017
1978	3,379	2,417
1979	4,055	2,936
1980	4,487	2,542
1981	3,339	3,539

Sources: 1946–76, H. Spraggins, "Rationalization of Rail Line Abandonment Policy under 4R Act," *Transportation Journal* (Fall 1968); 1977–78, "Rail Deregulation and Productivity" (Washington, D.C., Public Interest Economics Center, 1980), p. 32; and 1979–81, calculated from ICC computer printouts.

n.a. Not available.

Table 5-2. Results of Railroad Abandonment Cases Resolved by the ICC, 1979, 1980, and 1981

Year	Miles requested[a]	Miles granted	Miles denied	Miles withdrawn
1979	4,327.83	2,936.27	653.56	738.00
1980	7,068.68	2,541.75	68.29	4,458.64
1981	4,486.95	3,538.85	42.84	905.26

Source: Calculated from unpublished ICC computer printouts.

a. These figures differ from the "miles requested" figures in table 5-1 because they refer to the miles requested for cases *resolved* in the specified year, rather than to those actually requested in that year. A case resolved in 1980 might have been initiated by a railroad in 1978 or 1979. Table 5-2 thus provides a more accurate basis for comparison.

evaluation of the economic effects of deregulation—that should be the topic of subsequent studies. Nevertheless, scraps of evidence on the railroad industry in 1980, 1981, and early 1982 are available. And since many policies of deregulation were implemented before the passage of the Staggers Act, it is possible to draw some tentative inferences on the effects of deregulation from this period. As table 5-3 indicates, the most striking single occurrence in the industry in 1980 and 1981 was its increase in profitability. Overall, it earned a better than 4 percent return on investment for the first time in over twenty-five years (this is based on standard company accounts rather than the more elaborate calculations shown in chapter 1). And the return on investment went above 5 percent for the first three quarters of 1981—the highest return on investment earned by the industry in nearly forty years.

As the table shows, these higher profits are not the results of deferred maintenance or other postponed investments. On the contrary, the industry's maintenance and investment expenditures increased sharply from those of the mid-1970s. These results have important implications for the profitability results shown in chapter 1. They make it very likely that the more prosperous firms discussed there, while they failed to earn an opportunity cost of capital in the 1970s, may now be earning that opportunity cost, and that firms that were only marginally viable are now approaching financial viability. On the other hand, an overall industry return of just over 5 percent does not change the conclusion reached in chapter 1: that many firms and services will still have to be restructured if industry viability is to be achieved.

Some speculation about the role played by regulatory reform in these increased railroad profits may be useful. Once again, however, a definitive description will require further study.

Table 5-3. Rail Profitability and Related Evidence, 1975-81

Year	Return on investment (percent)	Capital expenditures on way and structures (millions of dollars)	New rail laid (tons)
1975	1.20	486.4	537,537
1976	1.60	549.9	802,441
1977	1.24	750.8	952,144
1978	1.52	855.2	838,714
1979	2.87	1,039.3	1,064,827
1980	4.25	1,275.0	n.a.
1981[a]	5.11	n.a.	n.a.

Source: Association of American Railroads, *Handbook of Railroad Facts* (Washington, D.C.: AAR, 1981). Also compiled in Don Phillips, "Right Track?" *Trains*, vol. 42 (April 1982), p. 6.
n.a. Not available.
a. First nine months only. From *Railway Age*, vol. 183 (February 22, 1982), p. 14.

The president of the Association of American Railroads cites two things as being instrumental in achieving the higher level of rail profitability in 1980 and 1981: rate increases and a shift in commodity mix toward more profitable commodities, especially coal and grain. In 1981 the industry instituted rate increases of over 14 percent, holding commodity mix constant. Because of the shift to lower-rated (but more profitable) bulk commodities, however, revenue per ton-mile increased about 10 percent.[16] These rate increases are in line with the analysis presented in chapter 4—rates rose from deregulation, but not very much, probably no more than 5 to 6 percent once inflation is accounted for. This is toward the lower end (but still within the range) of economic predictions.

But while the level of railroad rates did not seem to change greatly as a result of deregulation, perhaps the structure did. According to a survey of 2,200 of the largest manufacturing corporations made by Harbridge House, fully 23 percent of all responding shippers reported that rail rates had fallen, not risen, in 1980.[17]

Indeed, there was evidence in 1981 that rate wars were breaking out on some routes. The following quotation expresses the viewpoint of one Santa Fe executive:

Santa Fe favors deregulation. Santa Fe does *not* favor some of the things it sees happening since deregulation became a fact.

What Santa Fe sees happening in some instances—and it's not alone here— is that certain roads are using deregulation mainly to go after the traffic of other

16. Association of American Railroads, *Handbook of Railroad Facts* (Washington, D.C.: AAR, 1981), pp. 5, 9.
17. "The Harbridge House Survey of the Impact of Transportation Deregulation on Major U.S. Manufacturing Firms" (Boston: Harbridge House, June 1981).

railroads. . . . Jim Wright [Santa Fe executive] has a phrase for it: predatory pricing. And he doesn't like it—not just because it threatens to take price-sensitive business away from one railroad merely to give it to another, but also because he thinks it will in the long run threaten the stability of the railroads practicing it.[18]

Members of the sales departments of other railroads have also complained privately about the destructive competitive policies of their rivals. How likely destructive competition is to reduce profitability and weed out competitors in the future is unclear. But two things emerge from experience so far. First, while rate increases have undoubtedly played an important role in increasing rail profitability under deregulation, it is nevertheless clear that changes in the structure of rail rates have also played an important role. Second, the rate decreases (and rate wars) that have actually occurred cannot have harmed profitability too much. And the role of incentive rates, found to be important in other countries, cannot be understated either.

The effects of deregulation on abandonments seem unambiguous. The bankruptcies and liquidations of the Milwaukee and the Rock Island obviously leave the remaining roads in their areas in better financial condition. And the ICC's newer, more permissive policies toward abandonments, as well as the willingness of state and local governments to take over unprofitable services, must have helped improve the industry's finances.

The shift in commodity mix toward more profitable traffic is the likely result of deliberate decisions on the part of rail firms to price themselves out of markets that offer little profit and to pursue profitable traffic instead. This shift is therefore probably due to the greater freedom from common carrier obligations.

Economically desirable though the early results of rail deregulation were, some important unresolved issues still faced the ICC in its interpretation of the Staggers Act and, more broadly, in its policies toward intercity freight transportation.

Unresolved Questions in Regulatory Policy

Perhaps not surprisingly, the thorniest of these unresolved problems concern shippers of the most important commodity still carried almost entirely by rail, coal. The questions to be answered are those that are

18. *Railway Age*, vol. 182 (June 29, 1981), p. 28.

basic in economic regulation of any market: how high a rate level should be allowed, and to what extent should new firms, rail or nonrail, be allowed to enter the most lucrative markets for coal?

Coal Rates

Coal rates precipitated the most bitterly contested of any regulatory battle since regulatory reform of the industry. It started with a case in which the Burlington Northern attempted to raise rates on a shipment of coal to the city of San Antonio by including a charge for electric power generation, and the city sued to prevent it. The city found the ICC's decision in this case too favorable to the railroad and appealed it to the courts, which then returned it to the ICC. Meanwhile, the ICC broadened the case to encompass more general rate-setting guidelines, first for all coal in the western states, and then for all coal shipped by rail in the United States.[19]

The case dealt with a number of issues, all relevant to the level of coal rates, but by far the most important was that when rates were set at the maximum level permitted for market-dominant traffic, practically all railroads failed to achieve a return on investment deemed adequate by the ICC (or, for that matter, adequate based on the analysis in chapter 1). Since the Staggers Act emphasized the need for the industry to earn a compensatory return on investment, the firms wished to increase their rates on the commodities that could bear it (especially coal) to achieve a compensatory return. A set of rates on various commodities, adjusted to what the market will bear for each shipment but producing no more than a normal rate of return on investment, is the essence of second-best pricing.

Representatives of the railroads argued that, because Ramsey prices correspond to the most efficient possible prices that are feasible without subsidies but that still offer a compensatory return on investment, coal rate increases should be granted, at least to the point where the industry achieves a compensatory return on investment. The coal shippers argued that, while some differences in the ratios of price to variable costs are necessary and inevitable if the rail system is to be viable, Ramsey prices that placed such a heavy burden of achieving viability on them would be

---

19. Interstate Commerce Commission, *Ex parte* 347: Coal Rate Guidelines—Nation-wide—preliminary decision issued December 16, 1981.

unfair and discriminatory under the remaining common carriage provisions of the Interstate Commerce Act. Furthermore, they believed that allowing the railroads to raise coal rates without limits as long as earnings were noncompensatory would give them inadequate incentives to reduce costs elsewhere, either through more efficient operations or through elimination of unprofitable services.

Although the ICC had not made its final decision on this case by early 1982, it had nevertheless resolved some of the relevant issues in an interim decision,[20] largely favoring the railroads. For example, it ruled that railroads were entitled to base their rates on the current (as opposed to historical) costs of debt capital (in times of rising interest rates, current costs are much higher than historical costs). It also allowed railroads to recover a return on investment on deferred taxes, consistent with other public utilities.

But the most important opinion of the commission was on Ramsey prices: without committing itself, it suggested that it might well be inclined to support Ramsey pricing so long as it did not degenerate into pure cross-subsidization. In other words, the commission stated that as long as differential pricing was used to support common or fixed costs that would have to be paid for in a coal-only system, it might make sense. On the other hand, the commission noted that it would clearly be unfair to expect coal shippers, in the name of Ramsey pricing, to pay the fixed cost of a system larger than was needed for them alone. The commission therefore suggested that its next task would be to determine just what fixed overhead costs were genuinely needed for a given shipper.

This interim decision seems to make sense both legally and economically. From a legal viewpoint, the Staggers Act discourages cross-subsidization. From an economic viewpoint, any subsidization of unprofitable rail services is likely to be inefficient and undesirable, and in any event modest direct governmental subsidies are preferable to cross-subsidies.

The ICC's preference for line-specific costs also seems to make good economic sense, although it may be difficult to collect the necessary data. Indeed, if the ICC is able to develop its line-specific costing methodology correctly, it may find that on many coal-shipping routes Ramsey pricing is unnecessary to achieve a compensatory return on investment. Yet (as argued in chapter 3) on railroad routes operating at

20. Ibid.

greater than minimum efficient density, there is no evidence of scale economies, which would drop marginal cost below average cost. Furthermore, this minimum density is likely to occur between seven and fifteen net ton-miles per route-mile, depending on commodity type and other circumstances. Much (though by no means all) coal flows on routes at or above these densities.[21] Thus for a shipment of coal that flows exclusively on very high-density lines, the line-specific average cost should represent an adequate rate, and on lower-density lines, as actual traffic approaches optimal density, the need for Ramsey pricing should decline.

The main problem with such a line-segment-specific program of regulation is likely to be its complexity: doing a really effective job of controlling rates line by line would require much costly data as well as sophisticated costing methodology. Indeed, doing the job well is likely to require cost estimation at least as sophisticated as that of any study summarized in chapter 3, and perhaps more so. While this should be possible in principle, it may prove difficult in practice.

The alternative, which would allow the railroads to increase rates as they saw fit until they earned an adequate return, can also be defended economically: most important, railroads have no incentive to offer money-losing service, and since most of them are not currently earning an adequate return, they do have an incentive to pursue as many avenues as possible to increase that return. The number of abandonments sought in recent years is sufficient evidence of the industry's desire to eliminate money-losing services on its own. To the extent that it does so, it is unlikely that Ramsey pricing, which the railroads have requested in the *Ex parte* 347 case, will result in cross-subsidization.

Perhaps the most appealing compromise is that suggested by Mark Levin and Bruce Stram.[22] They argue that, for railroads that fail to earn an adequate return on investment, the ICC should allow a relatively gradual, year-by-year rate increase beyond the ceilings of 160 to 180 percent permitted by the Staggers Act. This would give the railroads a chance to test their demand curves slowly, and it would still give them plenty of incentive to eliminate unprofitable services because it would not allow them (even if the marketplace did) to achieve immediate

21. For a sense of the densities of coal flows in the United States, as projected to 1985, see National Transportation Policy Study Commission, *National Transportation Policies through the Year 2000* (Government Printing Office, 1979), pp. 454–57.

22. Mark M. Levin and Bruce N. Stram, "Nursing the Railroads Back to Health," *Regulation*, vol. 5 (September–October 1981), pp. 29–36.

revenue adequacy from rate increases alone. Finally, it would give shippers a chance to adjust to the rate increases, to seek alternative modes of transportation, or to try to contract with other railroads. As a railroad's rate of return reached a compensatory level, rate increases for captive commodities could be limited to cost increases. But if a policy that regulates maximum rail rates only loosely is to be successful, the entry of competing carriers must be allowed.

Entry of Competing Service for Coal

The entry of new railroads into a given market has for some years been a rare occurrence. Nevertheless, for lucrative coal markets, the incentive for construction of new railroad links can be considerable. One important case was that of the Powder River Basin coal area in Wyoming, which was served by a monopoly, the Burlington Northern. The Chicago and Northwestern, in a joint venture with the Union Pacific, applied for a certificate of public convenience and necessity to enter the market. Although the Burlington Northern opposed the entry, various coal shippers favored it; however, the issue had not been wholly resolved by early 1982.[23]

Although the entry of new rail firms into markets for coal transportation may be relatively rare, it should be encouraged by regulatory policy, especially rail policy that is permissive on rate ceilings. Such policies will help to make the markets for coal shipment contestable (see chapter 3) and hence help achieve lower, more competitive rates.

Another type of entry into the coal transportation market that should be encouraged is that of coal slurry, powdered coal suspended in liquid transported through pipelines. As this was written, Congress had not permitted slurry operators the eminent domain needed to build their slurry pipelines, the primary reason being pressure from the railroads against competition. The president of the Association of American Railroads stated that allowing slurry pipelines the needed eminent domain would "threaten the long-run economic viability of the railroad industry, which is the backbone of the nation's common carrier system."[24]

It has been argued that market controls to protect common carrier

23. Gus Welty, "Coal Traffic: It Just Keeps Rolling Along," *Railway Age,* vol. 183 (March 29, 1982), pp. 16–20.

24. "Slurry Lobby Calls in the Reserves," *Railway Age,* vol. 183 (February 22, 1982), p. 14.

obligations have been at the heart of many of the problems of the railroad industry and have caused many of the inefficiencies in intercity freight transport. It is ironic (but perhaps understandable) that the railroad lobby should resort to these same old arguments in an attempt to protect the railroads' profits.

In any case, it is difficult to find good economic justification for the AAR's position on this matter. If, as has been argued, railroads do not have a substantial cost advantage over other modes except for carrying coal, chemicals, and some bulk commodities, their raison d'être is threatened. To put things another way, it is no longer clear that railroads should (even in their own interests) serve as "the backbone of the nation's common carrier system," and it would seem strange to protect them from potentially more efficient modes for such a purpose. They should be given a chance to compete, so that the marketplace can decide. The competition from slurry pipelines, actual or potential, could well further limit the railroads' rate increases.

The issue of appropriate rate and entry regulation for coal is a complex one, and space here does not allow for a definitive solution. But a strong argument can be made for a market-oriented solution, which allows gradual rate increases at the discretion of the railroads up to a ceiling (such as 10 percent above the annual inflation rate) until the railroads achieve revenue adequacy. Such a policy should be combined with a permissive policy toward the entry of new railroads, slurry pipelines, and trucking companies in competition with railroads. But this conclusion is tentative.

Concluding Comment

As this was written, there was some doubt about how much of the legislative reform embodied in the Staggers Act and in the Motor Carrier Act of 1980 would actually be carried out. Still, there is much in these laws that will be difficult to modify through the enforcement procedure, especially in view of the strong start at deregulation made under the Gaskins regime.

In any event, one thing is clear. If the political system is willing to pay the price for freight deregulation (the ending of inefficient favors to special shipper and carrier groups), the Staggers Act and the Motor Carrier Act of 1980 afford it plenty of opportunity to improve the efficiency and productivity of its freight transportation system.

CHAPTER SIX

Further Problems
and Alternatives

OTHER public policy reforms besides the regulation of rail rates and abandonments could have a strong impact on the railroad industry and on the twin problems of inadequate profitability and inefficient resource allocation. These include taxation and subsidy policies toward railroads and competing modes, merger policies, labor practices, and other forms of institutional restructuring such as the separation of ownership of right-of-way from ownership of trains. Also, although it is not clear how public policy can affect it, "inadequate" management has been blamed for the railroads' problems. Finally, nonmarket, external considerations, such as energy conservation, environmental protection, and national defense, are sometimes cited as justifying government intervention in the railroad industry.

Many studies that analyze transport regulation give little attention to these issues. When they are included, however, care must be taken not to generate an inaccurate analysis of public policies. From a positive viewpoint, only by considering *all* aspects of public policy can we hope to understand the true causes and motivations. From a normative viewpoint, potentially conflicting and contradictory policies may be uncovered.

Subsidy and Taxation Policies toward Competing Modes

For some years, members of the railroad industry have argued that competition from the truck and barge industries is unfair because those two modes use publicly provided highway and waterway facilities whereas the railroads have had to provide their own rights-of-way, as well as maintain and pay taxes on them.[1] Of course, even the railroads

1. For the duration and flavor of these controversies, see John R. Meyer, Merton J. Peck, John Stenason, and Charles Zwick, *The Economics of Competition in the Transportation Industries* (Harvard University Press, 1959), pp. 64–85.

would not argue that public provision of highways and waterways was unfair if the users of those facilities paid the full costs of providing them, based on the same cost criteria as those used by the railroads in the private sector.

Hardly any question in transportation economics, however, has generated so much controversy over the years as whether truckers and barge operators pay the full costs of the facilities they use. It is well beyond the scope of this study to resolve that issue. Rather, the aim here is more modest: to determine whether any economically appropriate adjustment of user fees for competing modes would have a meaningful impact, either on allocation between rail and other modes of transportation or on the viability of the railroad industry itself.

The Trucking Industry

The nation's system of main highways (state and federal roads) is ostensibly supported by user fees. In most states these roads are supported by a system of taxes on fuel, tires, and other necessary adjuncts to driving. It is often argued that, because a large part of highway expenditures come from this fund, the nation's road system is self-supporting and that for this reason resources should be allocated properly between highway and other modes of transportation.[2]

There are several problems with this argument. First, it is empirically incorrect. In 1977, out of expenditures of $29.8 billion on the nation's highway system, $7.7 billion came from general revenues, that is, taxes other than user taxes.[3] This subsidy may be viewed as irrelevant to resource allocation because it is used to finance only local roads, especially urban streets. But such a view is fallacious: many vehicles travel over these roads, generating substantial user tax revenues. Generally, however, these revenues cannot be used to support local roads, so they are siphoned off to pay for the construction and maintenance of state and federal roads, including the interstate system. Thus urban taxpayers are subsidizing the nation's main intercity highway network. The justification for this is that urban residents benefit from intercity roads.[4] But such a policy could have a side effect of distorting resource allocation between intercity modes of transportation.

2. See, for example, John R. Meyer, John F. Kain, and Martin Wohl, *The Urban Transportation Problem* (Harvard University Press, 1965), pp. 60–63.

3. Federal Highway Administration, *Highway Statistics for 1977* (Government Printing Office, 1978), p. 118.

4. Meyer, Kain, and Wohl, *Urban Transportation Problem*, pp. 60–62.

Some who have studied this problem have a very different viewpoint. They argue that since most of the nation's intercity road system is uncongested, and since most highway capital costs do not vary with vehicle use, the intercity road system should not be expected to recover its "fully distributed" cost, or anywhere near it.[5] Setting user charges to recover "sunk" capital costs in the nation's highway system will simply underuse the highway system and waste resources. If its assumptions are granted, this argument is correct. Compelling though it seems to most economists, however, it too is somewhat flawed. The assumption that investment (or the need for investment) in the nation's highway system is largely invariant to use, especially by heavy trucks, is highly questionable. And wear and tear aside, there is strong and statistically significant evidence that capacity in intercity highways has been adjusted by highway authorities to accommodate changes in travel, with the idea of maintaining a given service level.[6] To the extent that highway capacity is in fact allowed to vary with demand, users of the highway system should pay for the costs of that capacity.

Finally, a much more pragmatic argument can be made for significantly higher user charges, especially for truck transportation. Evidence is now mounting that the nation's highway system is deteriorating for lack of maintenance expenditures.[7] It is widely agreed that highway expenditures will have to be increased to maintain this system in the future,[8] and since taxpayers in the United States appear unwilling to increase general revenue commitments for anything (save possibly defense) in the early 1980s, that makes an increase in user charges likely and necessary.

Even if it is granted that highway user charges should go up, how large an increase should be allocated to heavy trucks of the sort that compete with rail? The issue of highway cost allocation among various types of vehicles, especially to heavy trucks, is, if anything, even more controversial and further from resolution than the overall issue of whether highways are or should be subsidized. This is partly because of considerable disagreement on the theoretical criteria to be used in

5. A. A. Walters, *The Economics of Road User Charges* (Johns Hopkins University Press, 1968).
6. Theodore E. Keeler, "Resource Allocation in Intercity Passenger Transportation" (Ph.D. dissertation, Massachusetts Institute of Technology, 1971), chap. 3.
7. For an analysis of the extent to which maintaining the system might equitably fall on trucks, see, for example, Department of Transportation, "Second Progress Report on the Federal Highway Cost Allocation Study," January 1981.
8. "Despite Reagan's Tax-Cut Promise, 40 States Want to 'Up' Fuel Taxes," *Traffic World*, vol. 185 (February 2, 1981), p. 19.

allocating costs, and partly because, for a given theoretical allocation criterion, the empirical evidence needed to determine that allocation is ambiguous.

Everyone would agree in theory that each vehicle should pay for the marginal wear and tear it imposes on the nation's road system. But what of the fixed costs of the roadway itself? Some argue that each vehicle class should pay the extra cost of accommodating that class (for all highways but those designed only for private autos), such as thicker pavements, stronger structures, higher clearances, and the like. This approach has been traditionally used by the Federal Highway Administration in attempts to allocate user charges fairly.[9] Others argue that this procedure is highly arbitrary (the charges attributed to a given group depend critically on where the lines are drawn between vehicle size classes) and that it has no justification in welfare economics. Members of this group hold that a highway, being a joint product, has no cost-related method for allocating expenses. They argue instead that if a road system must cover its costs user fees should be based on second-best Ramsey prices of the sort discussed for railroads.[10] This procedure will allocate a relatively high proportion of joint costs to users with low demand elasticities while going relatively easy on users with high demand elasticities. (Such a tax system would tax truckers with close rail substitutes lightly, for these truckers would have relatively high elasticities of demand for highway use.)

I would argue (and have argued elsewhere[11]) that the long-run concepts of road pricing, wherein vehicle groups pay the incremental capital costs of accommodating them, will indeed lead to efficient resource allocation, and at the same time meet the criterion of fairness and help ensure (as Coase argues in his discussion of the desirability of average cost pricing[12]) that when an investment is made its benefits truly justify its costs. Finally, a policy of pricing based on long-run incremental costs is not nearly so inconsistent with optimal short-run highway pricing as some seem to believe.

9. Ibid., pp. 16–19.

10. Walters, *Economics of Road User Charges.*

11. Keeler, "Resource Allocation in Intercity Passenger Transportation," chap. 3. Also, short-run congestion toll pricing will generally cover long-run incremental capital costs of traffic. See Theodore E. Keeler and Kenneth A. Small, "Optimal Peak-Load Pricing, Investment, and Service Levels on Urban Expressways," *Journal of Political Economy,* vol. 85 (February 1977), pp. 1–25.

12. R. H. Coase, "The Marginal Cost Controversy," *Economica,* vol. 13 (August 1946), pp. 169–82.

Fortunately, however, it is not necessary to resolve the road pricing and cost allocation issue here. Rather, the question is simply whether any realistic increase in truck user charges, even some of the higher estimates, would affect the rail-truck competitive balance.

There have over the years been numerous estimates of appropriate truck user charges, and for the sake of argument I estimate from a source that, at the very least, has no incentive to understate charges that should be assessed on trucks—the Association of American Railroads, which in 1978 estimated the amount by which the trucking industry underpaid for its use of intercity roads at $1 billion a year.[13] Since the nation's total bill for intercity truck transportation in 1977 was $67 billion,[14] this implies that by the AAR estimates appropriate increases in truck user charges would raise truck rates by an average of about 1.5 percent. In considering this figure it is important to keep in mind that, as long as the rail rate is below the truck rate, the cross-elasticity between rail and truck transportation has been found to be quite low for practically all commodities. This further limits the ability of the railroads to benefit competitively from any realistic increase in truck user charges.

One other piece of evidence on truck transportation should add perspective. According to some estimates, the nation's truck freight bill had increased by about $3 billion a year as of 1972 as a result of truck regulation.[15] If truck deregulation is allowed (and there is plenty of economic evidence that it would be efficient if it did happen), its adverse competitive effects on the railroads would probably outweigh any favorable effects that an appropriate increase in user charges would have.

This result is roughly supported by evidence from Australia, where the highway system generates a substantial revenue surplus to the state and commonwealth governments, and the road system is somewhat more primitive than the one in the United States. Nevertheless, on main interstate routes, which have been deregulated (both truck and rail) since 1954, rail and truck market shares are roughly the same for manufactured goods as they are in the United States.[16]

13. Association of American Railroads Staff Studies Group, "The Economic Impact of Substituting Truck for Rail Transportation" (Washington, D.C.: AAR, July 5, 1978), p. 5.

14. Transportation Association of America, *Transportation Facts and Trends*, vol. 4 (Washington, D.C.: TAA, 1979).

15. Thomas Gale Moore, "The Beneficiaries of Trucking Regulation," *Journal of Law and Economics*, vol. 21 (October 1978), pp. 327–43, especially p. 342.

16. Theodore E. Keeler, "Regulation and Modal Market Shares in Long-Haul Freight

It is probably safe to conclude, therefore, that while large trucks should pay substantially higher user charges than they currently do in the United States, nevertheless more rational highway user charges would have relatively little effect on rail-truck competitive balances.

All the results here on truck user charges, and on the potential impact of a change in truck user charges on rail-truck competition, are quite consistent with the much earlier results of Meyer and others and of Friedlaender.[17]

Waterways

There has been a continuing consensus among economists studying the problems of barge transportation that the user charges paid for waterways are significantly below the costs of accommodating the barges. In fact, until very recently water carriers paid no user charges at all. The Congressional Budget Office estimated that in fiscal 1982 waterways users would fall $1.2 billion short of paying the costs of the service they used, and that if they were to pay these costs in full a fuel tax of about $1.30 a gallon would be necessary, rather than the actual tax of 4 cents in 1981, which is expected to rise to 10 cents by 1986.[18] This would more than double barges' fuel costs and would undoubtedly affect intermodal resource allocation.

Yet one may question whether an increase of $1.26 a gallon of fuel consumed would be efficient. The Army Corps of Engineers has, over the years, built many river navigation projects whose economic justification is dubious. In many cases these projects traverse areas with little traffic, and it is not even clear that their effects on rail competition are always strong. Charging all users $1.30 a gallon in fuel taxes would probably force those on relatively efficient, high-density channels, such as the Mississippi, to cross-subsidize "pork barrel" projects elsewhere. Ideally, of course, pork barrel water projects that have little commercial benefit should be abandoned or conceivably, if recreational benefits

---

Transport: A Statistical Comparison of Australia and the United States," in J. R. Nelson and H. O. Whitten, eds., *International Comparisons of Freight Regulatory Policy* (Washington, D.C.: Federal Railroad Administration, 1977), chap. 7.

17. Meyer and others, *Economics of Competition;* and Ann F. Friedlaender, *The Dilemma of Freight Transport Regulation* (Brookings Institution, 1969), pp. 34–52.

18. Congressional Budget Office, *Reducing the Federal Budget: Strategies and Examples, Fiscal Years 1982–1986* (GPO, 1981), pp. 53–54.

were great enough, supported by recreational user charges or even general revenues. But whatever is done about such projects, it is probably unrealistic to expect users of efficient waterways to support them. The question, then, is whether user charges are high enough on the higher-density, more efficient waterways—those that represent the most important competition to railways—and if not, what effect an appropriate change in these charges would have on rail-water competition.

The recent work of Daniel Boger answers some of these questions.[19] He estimated cost functions not only for firms using the Mississippi and Ohio rivers, but also for the provision of waterway services by government agencies in the area, and found that waterways users imposed on the government a marginal cost of slightly below 1 cent per ton-mile, almost none of which they paid in user charges. Nevertheless, incorporating evidence on rail costs from the work of Harris, he also concluded that inland water transportation would continue to enjoy a substantial cost advantage over rail transportation for the commodities it carries, even with the implementation of user charges at efficient levels.

Thus, while more rational pricing in waterways transportation would undoubtedly improve the competitive position of the railroads, it would have little effect on overall competitive balances.

Subsidy and Taxation Policies toward Rail Transportation

Although the railroads own (and pay corporate and property taxes on) some right-of-way capital, of which the counterpart in highway and waterway transportation is provided by the government, railroads do receive some subsidies. The most obvious of these currently are direct subsidies, accorded in the form of capital and operating grants to Conrail, which in 1981 totaled over $3 billion since its formation in 1976,[20] and subsidies to some of the less successful private railroads, under the Railroad Revitalization and Regulatory Reform Act of 1976 (the 4R Act), at a rate of about $500 million a year since that time. The government has also advanced substantial low-interest guaranteed loans to various "poor" railroads off and on going as far back as the Transportation Act of 1920.

19. Daniel C. Boger, "Economic Aspects of the Regulated Inland Waterway Freight Transportation Industry," Sloan Working Paper 7906 (University of California at Berkeley, Department of Economics, November 1979), pp. 117–43.

20. Congressional Budget Office, *Reducing the Federal Budget*, p. 81.

It is difficult to gauge the effect of these subsidies on resource allocation, except to note that a good part of them may have been wasted from the viewpoint of the taxpayer. Although the subsidies to Conrail have resulted in a substantial amount of useful rehabilitation of main lines of that railroad, they have also been used for an extravagant employee protection plan which guarantees any worker laid off with or after the formation of Conrail (who has been employed for five years or more) a lifetime pension at his most recent wage, plus whatever general wage increases occur over his lifetime.[21] And it is not at all clear that a large part of Conrail is needed for efficient resource allocation in transportation in the Northeast.[22]

Similarly, a large part of 4R money for rail rehabilitation has been spent on restoring routes of faltering railroads, such as the Milwaukee, the Rock Island, and the Katy, the economic justification for whose existence was questionable even when the funds were initially allocated.

As for low-interest loans, Hilton was probably right when he said they fulfill little function save to postpone the day when a carrier goes bankrupt, with more loss than gain to society in the process.[23]

Some railroads receive state as well as federal aid. This money is generally given out parsimoniously and earmarked for the preservation of service on very specific lines, with the amount negotiated between the railroad and the state government. The railroad supported this way is often a "short-line," or small, railroad that is exempt from the highly restrictive and wasteful labor practices imposed on the Class I carriers.[24] As a result, a significant amount of service can frequently be provided by relatively small subsidies. If subsidies to money-losing railroad service are deemed socially necessary, it can be argued that these locally supplied and specially targeted subsidies are the most likely to be efficient.

In addition to direct subsidies for money-losing service, all railroads

21. Staggers Act, title V.

22. The U.S. Railway Association has estimated that if Conrail were sold off to private railroads, they could profitably serve the 20 percent of Conrail's shippers that account for 80 percent of its traffic, using only 40 percent of Conrail's employees. See David P. Morgan, "On USRA, Mixed Emotions," *Trains*, vol. 41 (September 1981), pp. 3–7.

23. George W. Hilton, *The Transportation Act of 1958* (Indiana University Press, 1969), pp. 199–200.

24. For a discussion of short-line railroads, the aid they receive, and the work rules they face, see Pavan Sahgal, "Little Engines That Could and Will Again," *Venture*, vol. 3 (February 1981), pp. 70–72.

have received significant indirect subsidies over the years. The most widely cited of these are the land grants. Official federal land grants were given to only six transcontinental railroads. But there is plenty of evidence that thousands of miles of other railroad routing all over the country received similar land grants and other economic incentives from state and local governments. These grants now account for no more than sunk costs and should have little effect on resource allocation (of course, the same could be argued of the land now sunk in highway investments). It is true that many railroads may reap considerable financial benefits from the natural resources or other sources of high real estate values along their tracks. But even this will have no impact on intermodal resource allocation, because railroads have little economic incentive to use the profits from these natural resources to cross-subsidize their rail operations.

Another subsidy the railroads receive can affect resource allocation, however. That is the "betterment accounting" method, which allows railroads to write off investments in rails and ties for tax purposes in the year those investments are made, rather than depreciating them over time. Since rails last up to fifty years and ties twenty-five years, this rapid write-off reduces the railroads' corporate tax liabilities. Controversial legislation has been proposed that would force the depreciation of rails and ties for tax purposes. It is difficult to guess how important this would be. However, the tentative evidence presented in chapter 1 suggests that this effect, while it could be large enough to change annual rail profits by a significant amount (say, in the hundreds of millions of dollars), does not seem large enough to change the industry's return on investment or its long-term financial viability significantly. Further evidence, however, is needed to document this anywhere near conclusively.

Overall, though no precise quantitative evidence is available, there is probably only one way in which public subsidies to the railroad industry have affected resource allocation: they have encouraged the preservation of more services on more routes than the private market would support, and they have probably also increased operating costs, especially for Conrail. Elimination of these subsidies would probably divert a significant amount of traffic now carried on money-losing rail lines to truck. Paradoxically, the subsidies for rail construction provided in the nineteenth century may be having a perverse effect on rail profitability for some carriers now. Since they encouraged the building of more rail lines than would otherwise have occurred, they may account for the current lack of prosperity stemming from excess capacity.

The most efficient policies for current subsidies would probably be to drop systemwide programs, such as that for Conrail, and then to use specially targeted money, as the state of Iowa does, to fund service to specific shippers' communities where the benefits clearly justify the costs. The likely cost-competitiveness of truck with rail for low-density shipments, however, makes the desirability of keeping any service that the marketplace cannot support questionable.

Mergers

To proponents, rail mergers represent a way of both improving the efficiency of the transportation section of the economy and increasing the viability of the industry. Parallel mergers (consolidations of railroads operating on parallel routes) are often believed to have cost-reducing benefits because they may allow the consolidation of joint facilities and lessen maintenance on one of the two lines. End-to-end mergers, while they may produce some cost savings, such as consolidation of terminal facilities, are more often than not believed to improve service—more trains that bypass yards and better matching of schedules and rates to shippers' needs.

Opponents of rail mergers regard them as much less attractive. Most important, they see them as reducing competition, with few offsetting benefits. Obviously parallel mergers will reduce the number of competitors in a market, but end-to-end mergers will often have a similar effect because railroads that connect on some routes run parallel to each other on other routes. End-to-end mergers, however, can weaken competitors of the merged company in some markets through lost connections or better service on the merged line. Railroads standing to lose from such mergers usually protest them vigorously; the Union Pacific–Rock Island merger, for instance, was stopped by ICC indecision lasting for ten years, which was mainly the result of the protests of railroads that feared they would be hurt by the merger. Thus both parallel and end-to-end mergers can harm competitors in two ways. First, the merger can increase the market power of the merged railroad, raising monopoly rents or reducing managerial efficiency. Second, driving some competitors out of business may reduce the number of communities and shippers served.

Viewed in this light, a merger policy designed to protect competitors is equivalent to a policy designed to cross-subsidize money-losing services.

Now that the 4R Act and the Staggers Act give the railroads more freedom to abandon money-losing common carrier service obligations, it is appropriate to reexamine the whole issue of railroad mergers, as both the industry and the ICC have recently done.

The empirical evidence on the effects of mergers is suggestive but inconclusive. Various studies of parallel mergers indicate that the benefits they generate tend to be small. This is consistent with some early work by Gallamore,[25] and with subsequent results of Department of Transportation reports and of statistical work done by Levin and Weinberg.[26] Gallamore and the Transportation reports attempted to place dollar benefits on parallel mergers and were unable to find significant ones. The Levin and Weinberg study, on the other hand, examined market shares of the relevant railroads in a number of markets before and after the mergers and found that firms engaging in parallel mergers tended to lose or, at best, hold their market share. It should be emphasized, however, that the merging firms studied were not permitted to abandon one of the two parallel routes. Based on the results on economies of traffic density discussed in chapter 3, permitting such abandonments could make parallel mergers a more orderly and efficient way to reduce redundant capacity than forcing one or both of the firms into bankruptcy before allowing the rationalization.

There is more evidence that end-to-end mergers do confer efficiencies. Two studies, the one by Levin and Weinberg and one by Harris and Winston,[27] provide tangible evidence of the benefits of this type of merger. Levin and Weinberg found that firms engaging in parallel mergers were able to increase their market shares relative to two unmerged firms, and they attribute this to improved service. Still, the increased market share of the merged firms does not indicate how important these benefits are. The more ambitious study by Harris and Winston attempts to quantify them and finds that, by integrating the present systems into a set of competing nationwide systems, they could

25. Robert E. Gallamore, "Railroad Mergers: Costs, Competition, and the Future Organization of the Railroad Industry" (Ph.D. dissertation, Harvard University, 1969).

26. Richard C. Levin and D. H. Weinberg, "Alternatives for Restructuring the Rail-Roads: End-to-End or Parallel Mergers?" *Economic Inquiry* (July 1979), pp. 371–88.

27. Robert G. Harris and Clifford Winston, "Economics of Integration in the Rail Freight Industry," *Review of Economics and Statistics,* forthcoming.

be as high as $1 billion a year. However, the estimates of Harris and Winston are based mainly on evidence for manufactured goods and hence offer only a partial estimate of the benefits of rail mergers.

The work of Harris and Keeler also provides some indirect evidence on efficiencies from rail mergers.[28] Controlling for a number of other factors, they find that length of haul has a positive though rather weak effect on rail profitability. This is consistent with casual observation of railroads. Although one thinks of railroads as being more profitable if their hauls are longer, this is not necessarily true. The Pittsburgh and Lake Erie, a very short railroad, is highly profitable, whereas the Southern Pacific, with long hauls, is considerably less so.

Nor do end-to-end mergers necessarily guarantee the benefits of longer hauls. Of critical importance is whether there is enough through traffic to consolidate trains and skip yards, no matter what would happen without the merger.[29] Some firms with very long end-to-end mileage may have little through traffic; others, such as the Richmond, Fredericksburg, and Potomac, the Rio Grande, and even the Union Pacific, have managed to achieve very efficient run-through operations without integration of the firms. Nevertheless, especially with rate flexibility, an integrated firm can probably respond more easily to changes in the marketplace than can two unintegrated firms, which must renegotiate rates and service every time the market changes. This problem is exacerbated by the antitrust reform in the Staggers Act, which makes collective rate making more difficult and, perhaps more important, gives strong firms an excuse not to cooperate with weaker ones in making interline shipments.

Evidence indicates that parallel mergers are likely to yield efficiencies only if they are accompanied by the abandonment of substantial amounts of duplicate route-mileage. End-to-end mergers, on the other hand, appear to confer benefits in many cases, but just how important these benefits are is difficult to say.

The social costs of mergers are still more difficult to quantify. A policy of preserving competitors to assure the continued existence of money-losing service is inefficient, and the ICC seems to have abandoned it. Far more ambiguous is the question of whether railroad mergers should

28. Robert G. Harris and Theodore E. Keeler, "Determinants of Railroad Profitability: An Econometric Study," in Kenneth D. Boyer and William G. Shepherd, eds., *Economic Regulation: Essays in Honor of James R. Nelson* (Michigan State University Press, 1981).
29. The importance of this point emerged in discussions with A. Scheffer Lang.

be blocked so as to preserve economic competition. There is little evidence on this and even less consensus. Some who have studied the problem believe that intermodal competition is so strong that intrarail competition is irrelevant or nonexistent, and there is little point in attempting to preserve it. Others believe that intramodal competition is very important and will bring significant benefits to shippers and consumers. I believe that when there are too many firms in a rail market (that is, parallel lines with less than minimum efficient route density) destructive competition will result until one or more firms are driven out. But once this happens, especially if the number of firms remaining is small (say, two), prices and services will be coordinated, and as the firms approach or reach minimum efficient traffic density, the problem of destructive competition will disappear.

Whatever the effect of rail mergers on pricing policy, some generalizations can be made about their likely effect on the structure of major rail markets. Most rail markets today contain no more than three firms, and many contain only one or two (although that was not so until recently—six firms competed with the Chicago–Omaha line in 1960, but mergers and bankruptcies have cut the number in half). Most rail mergers under consideration would reduce markets to duopolies. In markets that include three firms, at least one of the firms is almost inevitably earning a lower return on investment than that classified as "marginally viable." The Illinois Central Gulf is the weak carrier between the Midwest and the South, the Southern Pacific is relatively weak between the Midwest and the Southwest, and the Katy is the weak carrier between Missouri and Texas. This does not mean that wherever there are three firms one should be driven from business, since with deregulation many of the weaker firms may be able to strengthen themselves. But it does mean that a merger policy attempting to preserve three-firm markets at the expense of economic efficiency may be inappropriate. It is difficult to find evidence that shippers in areas served by duopolies in Canada complain of high rates or inferior service—deregulated duopoly markets appear to have worked well.

The argument presented here is obviously speculative. But from what we know, it is difficult to see good reasons for blocking a rail merger with demonstrated efficiencies simply to preserve competitors, especially if the merger does not create a rail monopoly covering a significant area. From an economic point of view, a policy that encouraged pruning out weaker railroads might make the industry healthy and economically viable much more rapidly than a policy that prolonged the agony of weaker firms.

All the evidence presented here on railroad mergers is less than conclusive, however. Only further research and the test of time will tell how beneficial they are to society.

Labor Practices

The forced use of five-man crews and 100-mile days on freight trains, combined with the fact that the wages of everyone in the industry, from secretaries to mechanics, tend to be higher than elsewhere, would seem to exact a high price in both economic efficiency and level of industry viability.

Since line-haul transportation labor costs represent 26 percent of total rail operating expenses,[30] it is not difficult to imagine that a more market-oriented set of wages and work rules could have a substantial positive impact on the industry. But it is not just in the area of costs that such changes could be beneficial. The railroad industry is at a disadvantage relative to trucking because rail service tends to be slow and unreliable. One of the primary reasons for this, in turn, is that high crew costs make it necessary to operate long trains. Shorter trains can not only run more frequently than long ones, but they also make it more feasible to block trains to a single destination, bypassing yards and the delays that may occur there. The potential for improving service without increasing costs is probably at least as important as the potential for reducing costs to improve economic efficiency.

While it is easy to make an a priori case on the benefits of improved labor practices, it is much more difficult to find empirical evidence on how great those benefits might be. Smaller short-line railroads are usually free of these work rules, but the structure of their operations is so different from that of large Class I railroads that comparisons have little meaning.

One Class I railroad, however, has, after many years of labor strife, managed to rid itself of union work rules, wages, and labor practices— the Florida East Coast. It first defied its unions in 1964, preferring a strike to union wages and work rules. Staffing its trains with supervisory

---

30. Harris and Keeler, "Determinants of Railroad Profitability," p. 18.

and other nonunion personnel, it simply accepted a strike in 1964 which never ended. The railroad was unprofitable during the first years of the strike, its plant was vandalized, and workers sabotaged its trains, causing some deaths. Nevertheless, by the early 1970s the Florida East Coast had become a relatively profitable railroad.

Based on a data sample for the years 1972–76, Harris and Keeler found that the Florida East Coast was much more profitable than a "typical" Class I railroad would have been with the Florida East Coast's route density, size, and length of haul but without its work rules. The period for which the Harris-Keeler sample was taken was one of its more prosperous periods. Also, other factors may have affected its profitability, and these were not controlled for in the study. Nevertheless, these results strongly support the hypothesis that the reformed wages and work rules adopted by the railroad greatly increased its profitability and benefited its shippers.

Other Forms of Restructuring

From time to time it has been suggested that certain sweeping changes in ownership or management of the railroad industry could improve its efficiency dramatically.

The difficult financial situation of much of the industry might lead some to regard nationalization as a solution, presumably with the subsidies necessary to keep the system functioning well. Indeed, the United States is the only country in the world without a nationwide government-owned railroad system (Canada has one nationwide private firm and one public one, and other countries have almost exclusively government-owned systems).

Yet there seems to be little reason for a larger publicly owned rail system in the United States in the foreseeable future. A large part of the nation's rail system is financially viable, and there is every reason to believe that more rail firms will become so if they are allowed to reap the full benefits of deregulation. If Class I railroads do choose to abandon services deemed socially desirable, it is much preferable to form small, local firms to handle the needed traffic, even if those firms do receive government subsidies. The reason is simple: small railroads, which are not subject to the work rules and wages described in the preceding section, can be operated at a much lower cost than Class I railroads. In the aftermath of the Rock Island and Milwaukee bankruptcies, such firms have been successfully formed in a number of states, some receiving subsidies and some not.

There is no reason to believe that the body politic in the United States has any interest in more nationalized railroads. Amtrak and Conrail are viewed by the White House and Congress as drains on taxpayers' money, and efforts have been made to reduce their subsidies and to return Conrail to private ownership. Whether that occurs or not, all political evidence indicates that further nationalization is unlikely in the near future.

Another suggested form of restructuring is separating the ownership of right-of-way and train operations, possibly making the government the owner of the right-of-way and tracks.[31] This would have several benefits. First, it would put railroads on the same competitive footing as other modes. Second, the natural monopoly problem might disappear because the "fixed" costs would be covered by the government and marginal costs by the carriers. Third, it would increase competition, because many entrants could run their trains over the tracks, making for efficient rates, service qualities, and managements.

Although this proposal is superficially attractive, when it is examined in detail, it is much less appealing. First, a large part of the economies of traffic density in the industry are achieved by longer trains and better utilization of the equipment and crews associated with high densities, rather than by better utilization of fixed track. So separation of the ownership of right-of-way will not eliminate the natural monopoly problem completely, although it could lead to a more "contestable" natural monopoly. Second, as pointed out by Conant, rail technology is unlike highway and air technology in that it offers much less opportunity for one train (or vehicle) to pass another without stopping or slowing down, going in either opposite directions or the same direction. The result whenever the trains of one railroad operate on the tracks of another is often a bitter dispute about whose trains will get priority.[32] The potential for conflict rises considerably if the trains travel at different

31. These suggestions are summarized in D. P. Ainsworth and P. V. Stone, *Public Ownership of Railroad Fixed Plant: A Restructuring Alternative* (Greenwich, Conn.: Reebie Associates, 1979).

32. Michael Conant, *Railroad Mergers and Abandonments* (University of California Press, 1964).

speeds, as is inevitable with different degrees of service-sensitivity of traffic. Third, as pointed out by Meyer and others over twenty years ago, the separation of ownership of right-of-way for highways and airways has caused considerable problems, especially in congested areas.[33] And the problem of improper pricing for congested roads and airports has worsened significantly since the 1950s, when Meyer and his associates wrote about it.

There is, however, another form of restructuring that promises many of the benefits of separate ownership of trains and track without the costs—the system that has evolved in Australian interstate markets over two decades of deregulated rates and services, as described in chapter 4.[34] Although the railroads are ostensibly state-owned monopolies, much of the interstate traffic is carried by a highly efficient and competitive group of forwarders. Unlike American forwarders, which have been forced by regulation to consolidate only traffic consisting of less than carload or truckload, the Australian forwarders are in effect large multimodal transportation companies. All of them own trucking companies, which operate in deregulated markets on parallel highways. And one of the big forwarders, Ansett, also provides domestic airline and bus service. For their rail traffic, these forwarders charter unit trains, at prices and travel times negotiated freely with the railroads. The forwarders provide all the terminal and yard services, and competition among them is intense: they were as fast as or faster than American firms to adopt advances in piggyback and container technology.

The Australians have demonstrated that, even with state-owned railroad monopolies, it is possible to develop a highly efficient, competitive system of intermodal freight transportation companies. In the United States, on the other hand, Australian-type forwarders are apparently illegal, despite the passage of the Staggers Act and the Motor Carrier Act of 1980. Nevertheless, allowing them in this country would probably afford the best opportunity for restructuring the railroad industry efficiently.

33. *The Economics of Competition in the Transportation Industries*, p. 266.

34. See Stewart Joy, "Unregulated Road Haulage: The Australian Experience," *Oxford Economic Papers* (July 1964), pp. 274–85. See also Peter J. Rimmer, *Freight Forwarding in Australia* (Canberra: Australian National University, 1970); and Keeler, "Regulation and Modal Market Shares in Long-Haul Freight Transport."

Better Management

It is sometimes alleged that the railroad industry's fortunes and efficiency level could be improved by better management.[35] Yet it is difficult to separate the effects of regulation and the lack of incentives from what appears to be low-quality management. For example, when Stuart Saunders was president of the Norfolk and Western, he was widely regarded as one of the best rail managers in the country, but when he presided over the demise of the Penn Central, he was regarded as one of the worst. How, for example, is a profit-maximizing manager to run a company when it is being forced to give away investors' money to the point of bankruptcy and then exhaust its cash to provide services that have no chance of making a profit? Under these circumstances, a policy of "statesmanship" which does not appear to maximize profits may be consistent with the goal of extracting maximum compensation from the government when the corporation is nationalized. On the other hand, it might be optimal to minimize confiscation of investors' property by putting the least cash possible into the railroad and not worrying about managing it well, while transferring all possible resources into alternative subsidiaries.

This is not the place to analyze the behavior of the Penn Central management, and no claim is made that this speculation accurately characterizes it. The point is rather that as long as the railroad industry was forced to use investors' money to provide services without any hope of earning a positive cash flow, to say nothing of a competitive return on investment, there was little incentive to "manage" a railroad well in the traditional sense, and it would have been irrational to try. If, under deregulation, the industry is allowed to respond to economic incentives and eliminate unprofitable services, and if it is subject to the competitive pressures of the marketplace, it is difficult to believe that "bad management," whether real or illusory, will persist.

Energy, the Environment, and National Defense

When arguments are made about the desirability of taxing or subsidizing the railroads, nonmarket considerations are sometimes brought

35. See, for example, Daryl Wyckoff, *Railroad Management* (D. C. Heath, 1974).

into the debate. Since energy, the environment, and national defense include some externalities, reasonable economic arguments might be made for intervention in rail markets to reflect these externalities.

Because rail transportation is usually believed to consume less energy than highway transportation, it is sometimes argued that rail transportation should be subsidized to conserve energy. This argument would be supportable, at least conceptually, if regulatory policies held energy prices at artificially low levels. Then, extra-market efforts to conserve energy could in theory be justified. However, as by the early 1980s domestic energy prices were decontrolled and determined by the market, it is difficult to justify subsidizing rail transportation for conservation purposes. Furthermore, evidence on the energy efficiency of rail transportation indicates that, while generally rail is indeed more efficient than truck transportation, that is not always so. It depends on such factors as commodity type, length of haul, and route density.[36]

The environment is also given as a reason for subsidizing rail transportation: trains pollute less than trucks, and there are no appropriate effluent taxes on trucks. Again, however, the empirical basis for this argument is anything but well established. It can as easily be argued that intercity freight transportation is not responsible for an important part of the nation's pollution.[37] By its very nature, most intercity transportation occurs *between* cities in rural areas, not in metropolitan areas, where the major pollution problem is. Pollution seems an especially inappropriate justification for subsidizing low-density branch lines, which are generally situated in thinly populated, nonindustrial rural areas.

A detailed analysis of railroads and national defense may be found in a 1981 report based on a six-year study by the Department of Defense.[38] The aim of the study was to determine whether, in case of war, the country's rail network could move military freight and weapons, especially oversize shipments, between military installations, defense plants, major metropolitan areas, and airports.

36. A full discussion of the relative energy efficiencies of various modes may be found in Congressional Budget Office, *Energy Use in Freight Transportation* (CBO, 1982).

37. For a discussion of this, see Kenneth A. Small, "Measuring the Pollution Costs of Transportation Modes," *Journal of Transportation Economics and Policy* (September 1977), pp. 109–32.

38. Department of Defense, *A Study of Rail Lines Important to National Defense* (GPO, 1981). See also Don Phillips, "An Interstate Railroad System—Alias STRACNET," *Trains*, vol. 42 (April 1982), pp. 14–15.

The Defense Department planners developed a map of the rail lines deemed important for these needs (which they called the "strategic rail corridor network," or STRACNET). They found, first, that the chief requirement was a network of high-density, main-line routes—few branch lines or even low-density main-line routes would be needed. The entire STRACNET system is thus only 32,422 miles of main line out of a total system of nearly 200,000 miles. Second, they found that the railroads running those routes (privately owned except for a relatively small amount of Conrail trackage) had kept the system in better-than-adequate condition for the nation's defense needs. Indeed, only 233 of the 32,422 miles failed to meet the study's maintenance criteria, and those 233 miles were scattered about so much that they would "not have a major impact on the national defense."

In short, an exhaustive study of the nation's defense needs for rail transportation concluded that the existing system, largely market-supported, is more than adequate to meet those needs. Furthermore, since only a relatively small, core component of the nation's main-line route system is involved, any economic abandonments in the near future are unlikely to have much effect on the system. There is thus little reason for regulatory intervention.

Summary

A number of public policies toward the railroad industry other than regulation have been discussed in this chapter. Many of them have not only had an adverse effect on the industry, but have also distorted resource allocation. Distortions of this type result from subsidies for truck and barge transportation, labor practices, and attitudes toward mergers. Certain other policies have tended to subsidize the industry. Although land grants and other procedures designed to stimulate the industry's development in the nineteenth century were undeniably subsidies at the time, they probably no longer affect resource allocation. Current support of Conrail and the availability of low-interest loans and grants to financially needy railroads, as well as the "betterment accounting" system, which allows railroads to write off rail, tie, and roadbed investments as current expenses, are all subsidies.

The survey of the evidence provided in this chapter suggests that most policies of taxation and subsidization of railroads and their competitors have little overall effect on resource allocation between railroads and other modes or on overall rail profitability. In isolated cases, however, they have a strong effect, and imbalances should be corrected.

The analysis of mergers indicates somewhat inconclusively that end-to-end route integration has some benefits, although it is difficult to show that the effects are strong ones. On the other hand, parallel mergers are likely to produce few benefits unless the merger allows the abandonment of some duplicate route-mileage.

There are few potential benefits to be realized from more exotic forms of restructuring the industry, such as public ownership of right-of-way with private ownership of tracks. And there is little justification for government intervention in the industry's markets to further various externality-related causes, such as energy conservation, environmental needs, and national defense.

On the other hand, policies toward organized labor appear to be extremely important in improving the industry's efficiency. There is considerable evidence that both railroads and shippers would benefit significantly if rail wages and work rules were set by market forces rather than by compulsory arbitration of the demands of organized rail labor. Except in the regulatory areas of rates and abandonments, it is probably in the area of work rules and wages that public policy has the greatest opportunities to improve the efficiency and viability of the railroad industry.

CHAPTER SEVEN

Perspectives on Rail Freight Policy

THIS STUDY has two threads: a positive one, attempting to explain the reasons for observed public policies toward rail freight transportation, and a normative one, evaluating those policies by the criterion of economic efficiency and suggesting further appropriate changes.

In this chapter the threads are pulled together by reviewing the patterns of regulatory policy over the past century, showing how political and economic factors motivated the changes, and then extending the analytical model of regulation developed in chapter 4 to explain the full range of public policies toward railroads. It is shown in appendix D that the changes in regulatory policy observed over time are consistent with the theory of support-maximizing behavior.

But how does present regulatory policy compare with that which would be appropriate from a normative viewpoint? Is it efficient? If not, how might it be changed to achieve an efficient solution to the "railroad problem"? The second section of this chapter discusses economically appropriate public policies, based on all the positive and normative evidence accumulated in this book.

Past Patterns in Regulation

The legal principle of common carriage was in full bloom when rail technology was first developed, and it was applied to the industry, both in the initial charters granted the corporations and in the "fair and reasonable" rates that the courts, local communities, and state regulatory authorities required the railroads to charge even before passage of the Interstate Commerce Act of 1887. It is thus little wonder that research by Damus found that there were many "regulated" elements in rail rate structure before 1887. (These elements were mainly rates that appeared to reflect neither costs nor profit-maximization, but rather notions of fairness to various groups of shippers.)[1] From the birth of the railroad industry until 1920, common carrier obligations of rail service were enforced exclusively by state authorities.

Historically, rail regulation was not a matter of revolution, but of evolution. The 1887 act made many of the common law principles more specific, and it set up a single federal agency for consistent enforcement of the law. Yet its passage did not bring about a striking change—in the ensuing twenty years many of its innovative provisions were overturned in courts, and it took that long to pass legislation that would plug all the loopholes the courts found.

Nevertheless, the regulatory policies carried out under the act did have an effect. By the first decade of the twentieth century, farmers and small shippers had ceased to complain about discriminatory prices. The railroads no longer engaged in rate wars as they had in the 1870s and 1880s, and their returns on investment went up while measured risk to rail investors declined. The industry hit a high-water mark in this period.

The policies of the Interstate Commerce Commission also hit a high-water mark of effectiveness in meeting their goals during the decade before World War I. The railroads were profitable, investors were happy, and objections to monopolistic and discriminatory pricing declined.

Such a statement, however, makes implicit assumptions about what the goals of ICC policy were. In fact, they have occasioned considerable controversy. For years, one school believed that regulators generally attempted to set rates to control monopoly rents, affording customers of such industries as railroads and electric utilities the lowest and most efficient rates possible. This has been termed the "public interest theory" of regulation. A variant is based on the notion that many such regulated industries are subject to increasing returns to scale (as most of the railroad industry is likely to be) and that without direct public subsidies a "first-best" economic policy is infeasible. The theory of the second-best asserts that a regulator controlling an industry subject to increasing returns to scale should set prices so as to maximize welfare subject to a break-even constraint. The prices generated by such a theory, sometimes called "Ramsey prices," are similar to monopoly prices in that price-cost margins are inversely proportional to demand elasticities.

1. Sylvester Damus, "Two-Part Tariffs and Optimum Taxation: The Case of Railway Rates," *American Economic Review*, vol. 71 (March 1981), pp. 65–79.

Separate from and more recent than the public interest and second-best theories are economic theories of regulation developed by Stigler and Posner and extended to their highest level of refinement and generality by Peltzman. Like the second-best theory, the Peltzman theory predicts that price-cost margins will differ widely among users, and it gives the government special incentives to regulate industries subject to scale economies. However, it also predicts that price-cost margins will depend not on demand elasticities, but rather on the relative political influence of the various buyers and sellers in the regulated market. Besides integrating the Peltzman model more completely with consumer and production theory, in this book I have added the concept of extended service over a network, taking into account that the more profit a regulator has to work with, the more incentive he will have to cross-subsidize unprofitable common carrier services to increase his political support.

Evidence presented in chapters 2, 3, and 4 indicates that regulatory policies toward the railroad industry can much more readily be explained by the Peltzman theory than by the first- or second-best variants on the public interest theory. It is in this sense that it can be argued that rail regulation reached its high-water mark just before World War I. After the war the industry began to suffer increasing inroads from highway competition. The response of the regulatory process to the changes reveals much about that process and the goals of regulation.

To adapt, regulatory policy took two paths. First, it gradually relieved the industry of its common carrier obligations that highway competition had made unprofitable and obsolete. But political pressure never allowed it to grant these changes rapidly, so its second set of policies was directed at slowing the process of abandonment of common carrier obligations, both by regulatory fiat and by intervention in the marketplace in attempts to make continued operation of unprofitable services feasible.

This two-track policy was first evidenced in the Transportation Act of 1920, which placed rail abandonments under the jurisdiction of the Interstate Commerce Commission, removing them from the state authorities that had previously enforced the service provisions of rail corporate charters rigidly. The act also permitted the ICC to enforce minimum rates for the first time, to prevent rate wars, and to block entry of new railroads to protect existing carrier profitability; and it stipulated that the ICC encourage mergers of weak railroads with strong ones to keep service on the weak ones intact.

The 1920 act proved inadequate to stem the tide of intermodal competition: the rail rate structure was further eroded by truck competition, rail profitability suffered, and the industry's ability to support its full range of common carrier obligations continued to decline, exacerbated by the Great Depression. As a result, the Motor Carrier Act of 1935 and the Transportation Act of 1940 brought most highway and barge competition under ICC control, and the Reed-Bullwinkle Act of 1948 sanctioned the long-standing practice in rail and truck transportation of collusion among carriers to set freight rates. Furthermore, to protect the cartel the ICC began to use its powers of minimum-rate regulation vigorously, in some cases to the chagrin of the railroads that had first backed it.

As several railroads were on the verge of bankruptcy in the late 1950s, it was evident that existing policies were still not working. In response, the Transportation Act of 1958 further eased the railroads' common carrier obligations, transferring passenger-train discontinuance from state authorities to the jurisdiction of the ICC, as the Transportation Act of 1920 had done for freight. It also eased minimum-rate regulation. Both actions were a slight move away from the cross-subsidization of money-losing services. Yet the effects of the 1958 act were relatively minor. Furthermore, by the late 1960s and early 1970s, the industry's finances (and its physical condition as well) had deteriorated still further, culminating in the bankruptcy and cash exhaustion of several northeastern railroads such as the Penn Central and the subsequent bankruptcy of several midwestern carriers in the middle and late 1970s. These disasters brought about some changes in the 1970s that seemed dramatic although they merely accelerated trends begun in 1920.

First, public subsidy replaced cross-subsidies in the National Railroad Passenger Act of 1971 and the Regional Rail Reorganization Act of 1973. This is consistent with the earlier policy of intervening in the marketplace to preserve uneconomic but politically attractive service.

Second, the industry received relief from its common carrier obligations in the Railroad Revitalization and Regulatory Reform Act of 1976 (the 4R Act) and the Staggers Rail Act of 1980, which gave the railroads much more freedom both in rate setting and in abandonments.

Other public policies became somewhat more favorable to rail transportation in the 1960s and 1970s, paralleling regulatory reform. In the 1960s railroads were at last allowed to eliminate firemen from freight trains. In addition to the Florida East Coast and its hard-won victory on work rules, a few other railroads won labor concessions for certain types of service. Rail unions in the Northeast, threatened with the dissolution of Conrail, offered further concessions.

It appears that the cost of the decline of the railroad industry has been spread among rail investors, shippers that benefit from the obligations of common carriage (small shippers and those on low-density routes), captive shippers, and rail labor. When a number of firms ran out of cash in the 1970s, the cost-spreading process accelerated, resulting in both increased subsidies and regulatory reform. This spreading is consistent with an extension of the Peltzman theory of regulation: that the regulator maximizes his political support, which is a function of the benefits he confers on each group (labor, low-density shippers, captive shippers, investors, taxpayers, and so forth).

In appendix D it is shown that under the most plausible circumstances, the rational response for a regulatory agency faced with declining profitability in an industry is to spread the costs of the change in exactly the manner described above. The change is conceptually analogous to the behavior of a utility-maximizing consumer responding to a change in the price of a good or in income.

What about the future? The Staggers Act, for instance, may not bring as much relief from common carrier obligations as its initial proponents euphorically suggested. Part of Ronald Reagan's 1980 platform was that ICC truck deregulation had gone too far too fast, and upon election he appointed an ICC chairman, Reese H. Taylor, Jr., who held the old views on regulation.[2] Whatever Taylor's views are on truck deregulation, the evidence in chapter 5 suggests that his commission has substantially liberalized rail regulation since the passage of the Staggers Act.

In any event, whether it happens slowly or quickly, both the theory and the historical trends support the general prediction for the railroad industry of reduced common carrier obligations, somewhat higher rates for captive shippers, a slow increase in labor concessions, and, despite the recent swing of the political pendulum against subsidies for railroads, additional public support (though perhaps at the state and local level

---

2. As this was written, much of the evidence on Taylor's views was speculative. However, early in his chairmanship he appeared to have formed a coalition in the commission dedicated to reducing truck operating rights. This is far more consistent with the old ICC behavior than anything that has happened since 1979. See, for example, Albert R. Karr, "New ICC Chairman Reese Taylor Moves to Halt Trucking Industry Deregulation," *Wall Street Journal*, August 5, 1981.

rather than the federal) for unprofitable services that it is politically impossible to abandon.

Are these changes consistent with economic efficiency? In view of the political constraints outlined above, can rail transportation play the most efficient possible role in the U.S. economy?

Implications for Policy

Although public policy on railroads has unquestionably moved toward efficiency in recent years, it has always stayed well behind where it should be. For example, railroads in the Northeast were forced into a condition of severe physical deterioration as a result of regulatory policies that neither allowed them to abandon unprofitable services nor compensated them for providing those services. Service to shippers that would have been willing to support efficient, profitable routes degenerated badly and needlessly. The damage done by these policies was repaired at great expense to taxpayers for railroad rehabilitation. Similarly, the analysis in chapter 4 indicates that distortions in rates and the forced provision of uneconomic services cost shippers, investors, and the public as a whole at least $2 billion a year in the last half of the 1970s, and probably considerably more.

A large part of this welfare loss can be eliminated relatively quickly: there is certainly room for interpretation of the Staggers and 4R acts to allow for the needed policy changes, and much progress has already been made along these lines.

The most important policy change needed (and it has already been started) to achieve this result is the elimination of common carrier obligations to provide unprofitable services, including low-density lines, small shippers, disadvantaged ports and agricultural regions, and whatever residual of uncompensated passenger service the railroads remain saddled with. "Unprofitable" here is defined to mean earning a return on all marginal investments below an opportunity cost of capital.

The Staggers Act already contains provisions that, properly interpreted, would allow this to happen. It states that a railroad may not be forced to provide any service that fails to contribute to its "going concern" value—that is, fails to earn a market return on investment. There are, however, other provisions and opportunities for interpretation that could prevent market-oriented rail rationalization. First, stipulations on profitability are always open to interpretation. For years, in the case of both passenger trains and branch lines, the ICC's contortions of logic enabled it to interpret as "profitable" services in which few investors would wish to invest. Second, although procedures for abandonments have been accelerated, most of the old criteria are retained. If a railroad wishes to abandon service on a route, the burden still falls on that railroad to prove that the public convenience and necessity require or at least allow the abandonment. Of course, other parts of the act imply that the public convenience and necessity require that all activities of a railroad contribute to its going concern value, and the ICC under Gaskins did liberalize its abandonment policies. Nevertheless, there is still room for interpretations of the law that bend to political pressure for uneconomic service. Those favoring an efficient solution to the railroad problem have reason to hope that such interpretations will be avoided. Preliminary evidence on the implementation of the Staggers Act gives strong reason for optimism.

All this presumes more than the reader may be willing to presume— that the forced provision of unprofitable services is a bad thing. Yet freedom to eliminate unprofitable services through pricing changes or service discontinuances is a good thing for several reasons.

First, truck costs in the aggregate are very close to rail costs for most types of commodity. For services the railroads find unprofitable, rail probably has no cost advantage at all and, if relative prices reflected relative costs, would not be used. Under these circumstances, it is difficult to believe that rail service could pass a benefit-cost test even if it could not make money, theoretically possible though that might be in an industry with economies of scale.

Second, completion of the interstate highway system has reduced the net cost of lost service as time has passed. As pointed out by Lang, when small communities have lost rail freight service, the impact on their economies has been negligible.[3] Three other studies—one of low-density lines in Ohio, one of lines in Iowa, and one of lines in Manitoba—all came to the same conclusion.[4]

3. A. Scheffer Lang, "The Great Economic Leveling-Out of the Intercity Freight Transportation Market," in Kenneth D. Boyer and William G. Shepherd, eds., *Economic Regulation: Essays in Honor of James R. Nelson* (Michigan State University Press, 1981), pp. 55–64.
4. See Donald W. Larson and Robert C. Vogel, "Railroad Abandonment: Optimal Solutions and Policy Outcomes," in Boyer and Shepherd, eds., *Economic Regulation,*

Third, allowing the industry to abandon all unprofitable services offers the greatest opportunity for gaining concessions from organized labor on wages and work rules. This is because much rail service that is uneconomic at existing wages and work rules could become quite economic with more market-oriented labor practices. If labor were forced to choose between loss of jobs and more efficient work rules, it might well choose the latter. To some extent this has already begun to happen: as Class I railroads abandon routes, short lines often take over and operate the same lines profitably because they are not subject to Class I labor practices. And the threat of massive railroad liquidation can give organized labor an incentive to make concessions. When the Reagan administration pressed for the liquidation of Conrail, the relevant labor unions became willing to eliminate all pay increases over a two- to three-year period and to discuss work rule changes.[5] Once this process has begun, the competitive process tends to spread it to competing railroads, since one railroad will have difficulty keeping traffic if another enjoys lower labor costs and more efficient work rules.

It is of course possible that for social reasons a community (or set of communities) might want to keep and subsidize a railroad line that a Class I railroad did not want to keep and that even a smaller operator would not operate without subsidy. Even so, it is likely to be more economical to subsidize small short-line railroads at the state or local level than to try to keep a large, money-losing Class I carrier in operation with federal subsidies. Due has argued persuasively that state rail programs, subsidizing relatively small railroads, can be efficient.[6]

Rate deregulation will encourage this rationalization of railroad services, not only because it will allow the carriers to price themselves out of some uneconomic markets and more vigorously pursue others, but also because, paradoxically, rate wars if they occur will have the salutory effect of driving redundant firms out of markets, strengthening the ones that remain. This does not of course imply that all the services of a

---

pp. 65–82; George W. Ladd and Dennis R. Lifferth, "An Analysis of Alternative Grain Distribution Systems," *American Journal of Agricultural Economics,* vol. 57 (August 1975), pp. 420–30; and Edward W. Tyrchniewicz and Robert J. Tosterud, "A Model for Rationalizing the Canadian Grain Transportation and Handling System on a Regional Basis," *American Journal of Agricultural Economics,* vol. 55 (December 1973), pp. 805–13.

5. *Trains,* vol. 41 (June 1981), pp. 7–9.

6. John F. Due, "State Rail Plans and Programs," *Quarterly Review of Economics and Business,* vol. 19 (Summer 1979), pp. 109–30.

redundant firm will be terminated when it goes out of business. Stronger firms will buy up the routes that are still profitable, or the losing firm will restructure itself to provide only profitable services.

Similarly, a merger policy no longer obsessed (as the ICC was for many years) with protecting weak firms will also work to free weaker firms of uneconomic common carrier obligations. This does not mean that the ICC should deliberately pursue a merger policy designed to bankrupt any firm, but simply that, in considering a merger for which real economic benefits of any size have been demonstrated, it should not block that merger merely to preserve weak firms.

While this analysis strongly indicates that the railroad industry should be free of its common carrier obligations to provide unprofitable services, it does not suggest that all aspects of the principles of common carriage be eliminated. For instance, most shippers may prefer that the carrier assume liability for the delivered goods. In some cases, such as dangerous chemicals, social externalities demand that the carrier be held liable for damages. On the other hand, the contract rates provision of the Staggers Act allows some shippers to free themselves from paying for insurance against loss and damage. These reforms are probably appropriate.

Other components of the old law of common carriage would be preserved under antitrust laws pertaining to all trade, and they should be preserved. For example, if a railroad has space available on its trains and a shipper wishes to ship something at the published rate for that shipment, the carrier should not have the right to refuse service. Similarly, if a railroad offers bulk contract rates to a large shipper, it should also be ready to offer the same rates to a forwarder. The evidence from Australia indicates that competition among forwarders that operate in this way has been indispensable in ensuring that small shippers reap the benefits of deregulated competition. Although small shippers will not receive special favors, neither will they suffer from adverse discrimination: they need pay no more than the rates that large shippers pay, plus the extra costs incurred by the forwarder in collecting the small shipments (this assumes that the forwarding industry would be competitive under deregulation; evidence from Australia strongly supports this). Such competition among forwarders is apparently not now legal in the United States, and it is a reasonable guess that many railroads would oppose making it so. But if the railroad industry is to be freed of its common carrier obligations to provide unprofitable services, it is only fair that the small shipper be guaranteed the protection of the marketplace. After all, competition among retailers ensures that individual purchasers of, say, groceries are not discriminated against in favor of larger purchasers of food. In Australia freight forwarders play the same role for shippers as supermarkets do for buyers of food. This should be allowed in this country.

In the area of rates, the most controversial topic is maximum-rate regulation, especially for coal. Those favoring it point to the problems of captive shippers, both of coal and of other relatively profitable bulk commodities. Those who oppose it argue that the competition from coal slurry, changing locations of power plants, trucks, and other direct and indirect competitors eliminate this problem. Imperfect though the revenue adequacy provisions of the Staggers Act are, they do appear to represent a workable method of achieving maximum-rate regulation that both allows the industry a compensatory return on investment and blocks unreasonably high rates.

In the likely event, however, that the automatic rate ceilings specified by the Staggers Act fail to afford railroads an adequate return on investment, the best policy is probably one of allowing rates to rise gradually above these ceilings while monitoring their effects (and those of other moves toward rationalization) on the industry's return on investment. But the issue of maximum rates is a thorny one, which will probably not be resolved for some time.

Another topic is joint rate setting. In principle, the Staggers Act allows joint rate setting among firms making end-to-end connections, but not among parallel firms. However, a number of firms, fearing prosecution since they compete with firms on some routes and connect with them on others, have indicated a desire to avoid joint rate setting as far as possible. This law could be used by large firms, especially interregional ones resulting from mergers, to refuse to meet with some of their smaller connecting firms to set joint rates. How much of a competitive problem this will create remains to be seen.

The United States, however, is the only country in the world that is attempting intrarail competition without any collective rate making— even in Canada the two major carriers are free to collude on rates. Although in many cases, this pro-competitive policy could result in rate stability, that would not always be true. Such a policy would work only if policymakers were ready to tolerate rate wars. If they did break out, the number of firms on a given route should fall until the rate instability ended.

Finally, there are a number of rail firms, accounting for roughly half the traffic currently carried, that at least come somewhere near earning an opportunity cost of capital for their incremental return on investment. If these firms are allowed to rationalize their operations in the manner described in this study, the industry should continue to be able to handle a substantial amount of freight without public subsidies. Early experience under the Staggers Act supports this view. (Less profitable firms will either have to restructure their operations more drastically or go out of business.)

Freed of its medieval shackles of common carrier service obligations, the railroad industry should continue to play an important and profitable role in the U.S. economy for many years to come.

Calculating Returns on Investment

THE theoretically correct method is to calculate a return with annuity depreciation by solving the following equation for the net return r_n:

$$r_g = \frac{r_n}{1 - e^{-rL}},$$

where r_g is the gross return (including depreciation) on gross assets (including depreciation reserve in base), and L is the expected lifetime of the capital good or investment in question. As Feldstein and Summers have shown,[1] for long lifetimes (over twenty years), r_g and r_n are very nearly equal, so r_g is used in all my calculations.

Returns of All Nonfinancial Corporations

Book value calculations were done using Internal Revenue Service, *Statistics of Income for Corporations* for the years 1946–75. The basis for the calculations was:

$$r_g = \frac{\pi + d + t}{A + D},$$

where π is total annual profits for all corporations except financial ones before federal income taxes, d is annual depreciation, t is state and local government taxes, A is total firm assets as listed in *Statistics of Income*, and D is total depreciation reserve in the capital account.

Rates of Return for Railroads Based on Book Values

These were calculated from Interstate Commerce Commission, *Transport Statistics*, volume 1: *Railroads* for 1946–79. The accounts and

1. Martin Feldstein and Lawrence Summers, "Is the Rate of Profit Falling?" *Brookings Papers on Economic Activity, 1:1977*, pp. 225–27.

Table A-1. Railroad Accounts

Variable	Symbol	ICC account number[a]
Net railway operating income	Y	111
Federal income taxes	T	105
Taxes other than federal	T_L	110
Income from lease of road and equipment	L_R	135
Rent from leased road and equipment	LE	157
Road property depreciation	D_p	298
Equipment depreciation	DE	336
Current assets	A_c	14
Current liabilities	L_c	55
Total road and equipment property	K_p	23
Improvements on all leased property	IL	24

a. From Interstate Commerce Commission, *Transport Statistics*, vol. 1: *Railroads* (Government Printing Office, 1972).

their symbols are given in table A-1, along with the ICC numbers corresponding to the accounts. The formula for calculating the gross returns is

$$r_g = \frac{Y + T + T_L + L_R - LE + D_p + DE}{A_c - L_c + K_p + IL}.$$

Rail Returns Based on Replacement Values, with Rails and Ties Not Depreciated

These calculations were based on data for each firm from *Moody's Transportation Manual*, 1948–80. The formula for the gross return is once again

$$r_g = \frac{\text{cash flow}}{\text{gross value of assets}},$$

where cash flow is the same as the book value calculations.

The gross replacement of assets for year t is defined as

$$GV_t = \sum_{t-25}^{t} p_i IP_i + e_i IE_i + S_t,$$

where S_t is total value of train supplies and materials in year t, IP_i is new investment in road property in year i, IE_i is new investment in equipment for year i, and p_i and e_i are appropriate price deflators for rail structures and equipment, respectively, from the National Income and Product Accounts. For some years, the index was available only for structures and equipment combined; it was then applied to the sum of equipment and structures investments.

Rail Returns Based on Replacement Values, with Rails and Ties Depreciated

These calculations are identical to those of the previous section, with the following change:

$$r_g = \frac{\text{cash flow} + \text{rail expenses} + \text{tie expenses}}{\text{gross value of assets} + \text{gross value of rails and ties}}.$$

Gross value of rails and ties for year t is calculated by the following formula:

$$URT = \sum_{t-25}^{t} p_{Rt}R_i + p_{Tt}T_i,$$

where R_i is the number of tons of rail laid in year i, T_i is the number of crossties laid in year i, p_{Rt} is the average cost of a ton of rail in year t, and p_{Tt} is the average cost of a crosstie in year t.

A Survey of Studies
of Scale Economies

THE first systematic statistical analysis of the relationship between marginal and average costs in the railroad industry was made, appropriately enough, by the staff of the Interstate Commerce Commission in the late 1920s. It was done to determine the relationship between full costs and variable, or out-of-pocket, costs.[1] Working with a cross section of U.S. railroads, the ICC staff first allocated costs between freight and passenger service for each road, based on accounting techniques. Overhead costs not directly related to either freight or passenger service they allocated between the two based on gross ton-miles of service. They then estimated the following equation for freight and passenger service alike:

$$TC/T = a + b(Q/T).$$

This is algebraically equivalent to $TC = aT + bQ$, where TC is total allocated costs, T is track-mileage, and Q is gross ton-miles of service involved. The coefficient b is then a measure of the variable, or out-of-pocket, costs for the traffic involved.

This procedure, while quite advanced for the 1920s and 1930s, has since been found to have some problems. First, the use of gross ton-miles to allocate overhead costs between freight and passenger service significantly overstates the costs of freight service and understates the costs of passenger service. Second, the ICC specification did not allow for any fixed costs other than those associated with track mileage. Third,

1. Descriptions and critiques of the old ICC Form A costing methods may be found in John R. Meyer, Merton J. Peck, John Stenason, and Charles Zwick, *The Economics of Competition in the Transportation Industries* (Harvard University Press, 1959), app. A. See also Ann F. Friedlaender, *The Dilemma of Freight Transport Regulation* (Brookings Institution, 1969), app. A; and Zvi Griliches, "Cost Allocation in Railroad Regulation," *Bell Journal of Economics*, vol. 3 (Spring 1972), pp. 26–41.

in applying the results of these equations to find the variable costs of a given service, the ICC staff calculated the total variable costs as a fraction of total costs from the equation for an average-sized railroad in its sample and then applied that "percent" variable to all railroads in determining out-of-pocket costs. Obviously, by this formula, percent of costs variable will differ greatly from route to route and from firm to firm. Even with this less than perfect equation, the ICC could have made much more accurate estimates of variable costs than it did by assuming an appropriate percent of costs variable based on the actual traffic density for the rate in question.

The work of Meyer and his associates, published in several articles and a book between 1957 and 1961, advanced the ICC approach in several ways.[2] They estimated railroad costs in a number of different cost accounts, and specifications differed depending on the accounts estimated. However, most equations took on the following sort of specification:

$$TC = a + bQ_f + cQ_p + dS,$$

where TC is total costs, Q_f is a measure of freight traffic (usually gross ton-miles), Q_p is a measure of passenger traffic (also usually gross ton-miles), and S is a measure of size, usually track-miles.

This specification is obviously superior in that it allows for differences in costs between freight and passenger service, but it came in for another criticism by Borts, who argued that over the long run firm size should be a function of traffic level, so to estimate a long-run cost function, one should exclude the size variable. Inclusion of the size variable, on the other hand, should be consistent with a short-run cost function.[3] Meyer and Kraft did reestimate their equations with and without the size variables, and they argued that the short-run costs, as estimated with the size variable, should be appropriate low-density, single-track railroads that did not have enough traffic to "fill" the track capacity.[4] On the other hand, costs estimated without the size variable would be more appropriate for railroads with multiple-track operation.

2. For example, John R. Meyer and Gerald Kraft, "The Evaluation of Statistical Costing Techniques as Applied in the Transportation Industry," *American Economic Review*, vol. 51 (May 1961, *Papers and Proceedings, 1960*), pp. 313–35.
3. George Borts, "Statistical Cost Functions—Discussion," *American Economic Review*, vol. 48 (May 1958, *Papers and Proceedings, 1957*), pp. 235–38.
4. Meyer and Kraft, "Evaluation."

In essence, Meyer and Kraft were arguing that, for railroads that had reached minimum efficient traffic densities, "long-run" costs based on equations estimated without size variables should be used. However, if most railroads have not reached minimum efficient traffic densities, this approach is likely to generate upward-biased estimates of costs for firms that have reached minimum efficient density. Furthermore, because this approach confuses returns to firm size and returns to traffic density, it provides reliable estimates of neither. Indeed, every study that has come to the conclusion that there are no scale economies in the railroad industry has based its analysis on this confused specification, or a log linear equivalent of it. Such studies include those of Griliches and Hirschey.[5]

The next study of railroad costs was made by Borts.[6] He did a statistical cross sectional analysis of variance of freight costs for Class I U.S. railroads, based on data from the 1950s. He measured the existence of economies of density as follows: first, he divided the firms in his sample into classes by size; second, he performed covariance analysis on the entire sample so as to estimate within-class and between-class cost elasticities. He then interpreted the within-class elasticity to be the short-run cost elasticity, that is, the elasticity holding firm size (as measured by route-mileage) constant. He assumed the between-class elasticity to be the long-run elasticity: as output shifts among firm size classes, firms have fully adjusted all factor inputs needed to produce given outputs. If the cost elasticity holding firm size constant was below the elasticity allowing firm size to vary, that would be evidence of economies of density. Diseconomies of density would occur if the cost elasticity holding firm size constant were greater than the elasticity allowing firm size to vary.

Borts's results indicated some economies of traffic density for southern and western firms, but diseconomies of density for firms in the East. While there are some conceptual problems with his model,[7] the main problem is that he used the ICC method for allocating freight and

---

5. Griliches, "Cost Allocation"; and Mark John Hirschey, "Estimation of Cost Elasticities for Light Density Railroad Freight Service," *Land Economics*, vol. 55 (August 1979), pp. 366–78.

6. George H. Borts, "The Estimation of Rail Cost Functions," *Econometrica*, vol. 28 (January 1960), pp. 108–31.

7. See Theodore E. Keeler, "On the Economic Impact of Railroad Freight Regulation," Sloan Working Paper 7601 (University of California at Berkeley, Department of Economics, September 1976).

passenger costs. Since this method overstates freight costs and under-states passenger costs, the more passenger-intensive a railroad, the more upward-biased its costs in the Borts sample. Recall Borts's result that there are economies of traffic density in the South and West but diseconomies in the East. Probably in the 1950s, when there was much more passenger service than at present (especially in the East), the roads with the highest freight traffic densities also had the greatest amount of passenger service. Borts's results of diseconomies of freight traffic density in the East can thus be explained by errors in his dependent variable introduced by his allocation of costs between freight and passenger service. That this bias is the fatal flaw in Borts's results is confirmed by the work of Friedlaender, who allowed for different cost coefficients for freight and passenger service and, using substantially the same methods as Borts, found increasing returns to traffic density on most U.S. railroads.[8]

The next study of scale economies in the railroad industry was that of Healy, who dealt explicitly and directly with economies of traffic density.[9] He found that up to a density of about 3 million revenue ton-miles of freight per mile of road there are substantial economies. Above this, he found no such economies. Furthermore, he noted that all eastern railroads, plus the two largest western ones, had reached this traffic density on a system basis. Although some main lines in the country may have realized these economies of density, as Healy points out, most route-mileage in the United States had not and still has not reached constant return to density, and it is misleading to infer from Healy's results that there are no meaningful economies of traffic density in the railroad industry. In any event, problems in allocating costs and revenues between freight and passenger service seem to have biased Healy's results as they did those of Borts. Rather than comparing costs and traffic density, Healy relates firm *profits* to total traffic density, and his output figure is total *revenues* from both freight and passenger service. Now, it can be argued that in the 1950s passenger losses were a very serious problem for many high-density railroads in the United States, and high-density freight lines were also likely to have passenger service.

8. Ann F. Friedlaender, "The Social Costs of Regulating the Railroads," *American Economic Review*, vol. 61 (May 1971, *Papers and Proceedings, 1970*), pp. 226–34.

9. Kent T. Healy, "The Merger Movement in Transportation," *American Economic Review*, vol. 52 (May 1962, *Papers and Proceedings, 1961*), pp. 436–44.

Healy's analysis will therefore understate economies of density for freight-service-only operations.

In studies made in 1967 and 1974 I found substantial economies of traffic density in the railroad industry.[10] Based on Cobb-Douglas technology, cost functions were estimated incorporating the following arguments:

$$TC = F(Q_f, Q_p, T),$$

where, as before, TC is total costs, Q_f is gross ton-miles of freight, Q_p is gross ton-miles of passenger service, and T is track-mileage. To estimate the minimum efficient density, the expression above is differentiated by T, and the derivative is set equal to zero. Solving this expression of T generates the optimal relationship between trackage and output, or the optimal density. Substituting that expression for T back into the short-run cost equation will generate the long-run cost function past minimum efficient density. These studies also provided strong evidence of constant returns to firm size.

These studies can rightly be criticized because the most appropriate measure of traffic density should be in net ton-miles per route-mile rather than gross ton-miles per track-mile. This is because the actual traffic is tons carried, not including the weight of the train, and railroads are constrained (by indivisibilities and regulation) to operate route-miles rather than track-miles. By applying average measures of net ton-miles per gross ton-mile and track-miles to route-miles (track-miles include yard track, sidings, and so forth, and route-miles do not), my results can be converted to that basis.[11] Doing this results in a minimum efficient density of 15 million net ton-miles per route-mile.

A more direct approach, however, is to measure freight traffic in net ton-miles and density in route-miles, and to estimate the cost of production equations on that basis. Harris and Miller estimated cost functions of the following sort (Harris confined his sample to freight-service-only

---

10. Theodore E. Keeler, "Railroad Cost Functions: An Empirical Study" (B.A. thesis, Reed College, May 1967); and Keeler, "Railroad Costs, Returns to Scale, and Excess Capacity," *Review of Economics and Statistics,* vol. 56 (May 1974), pp. 201–08.

11. These computations are done in Robert G. Harris, "Rationalizing the Rail Freight Industry: A Case Study in Institutional Failure and Proposals for Reform," Sloan Working Paper 7705 (University of California at Berkeley, Department of Economics, September 1977), p. 53.

railroads, thereby eliminating cost allocation problems between the two service types):[12]

$$TC = a + bTM_f + cT_f + dR,$$

where TM_f is net ton-miles of freight service, T_f is net tons of freight service, and R is route-miles. While this approach does not generate a specific minimum efficient traffic density, nevertheless Harris's average cost curve looks very much like mine, and differences between average and marginal costs become negligible at roughly the same density: 8 million net ton-miles per route-mile. Harris's work also found increasing returns to length of haul.

Practically all the studies mentioned so far are based on estimated cost functions. But the work of Levin is based instead on an estimated railroad investment function, derived from Cobb-Douglas technology.[13] Using very different methods from previous studies, Levin also found strong evidence of increasing returns to traffic density.

Although the studies of Harris, Keeler, and Miller generate reasonably consistent results, they still have some shortcomings that subsequent studies have been designed to improve on. First, the synthetic approaches of Harris and Miller do not allow either for cross sectional variation in factor prices or for specification of the underlying technology. Second, the Keeler and Levin studies assume relatively restrictive Cobb-Douglas technology, and mine assumes that way-and-structures capital implicitly varies optimally with trackage. I also fail to allow for cross sectional variation in factor prices (although when wage variables were included in those equations, they were insignificant and very small in coefficient, evidently resulting from insufficient wage variations over the sample).

Three recent cross sectional studies, by Caves, Christensen, and Swanson, by Friedlaender and Spady, and by Harmatuck, have attempted to rectify these problems.[14] They were based on a more general

12. Robert G. Harris, "Economies of Density in the Railroad Freight Industry," *Bell Journal of Economics,* vol. 8 (Autumn 1977), pp. 467–82; and Edward Miller, "Economies of Scale in Railroading," *Proceedings—Fourteenth Annual Meeting, Transportation Research Forum,* vol. 14, no. 1 (1973), pp. 683–701.

13. Richard C. Levin, "Regulation, Barriers to Exit, and Railroad Investment Behavior," in Gary Fromm, ed., *Studies in Public Regulation* (MIT Press, 1981), pp. 181–224.

14. Douglas W. Caves, Laurits R. Christensen, and Joseph A. Swanson, "Productivity Growth, Scale Economies, and Capacity Utilization in U.S. Railroads, 1955–74," *American Economic Review,* vol. 71 (December 1981), pp. 994–1002; Ann F. Friedlaender and

form of technology, as specified in the translog cost function, which makes the logarithms of costs quadratic in the logarithms of outputs and factor prices. Friedlaender and Spady also attempted to overcome the second problem, which stems from my assumption that way-and-structures capital and trackage are being varied in an optimal way (relaxing this assumption is especially useful in the case of capital-starved railroads, which have been unable to optimally adjust way-and-structures capital to trackage provided). Friedlaender and Spady allow for separate effects of way-and-structures capital, and they calculate optimal long-run costs for a given amount of route-mileage.[15]

All the studies based on neoclassical production functions generate estimates of minimum efficient traffic density. The studies based on "synthetic" specification, those of Miller and Harris, while they do not present estimates of minimum efficient density, do give some indication of the percent of costs variable, both for a given density and for a "typical" mile of route, as do the studies based on neoclassical specifications. It is instructive to compare the results of these studies.

The minimum efficient traffic density for a freight-service-only route in my 1974 study would, as already stated, be around 15 million or more net ton-miles per route-mile. Evaluated at mean route density, that study generated a "percent of costs variable" of 56 percent, based on the route structure and costs existing in 1969.[16]

The Harris study for 1969 traffic densities generates a percent of costs variable of 60 percent.[17] Although it is not specified to generate a minimum efficient traffic density, the Harris cost function flattens out only at extremely high traffic densities. At 30 million net ton-miles per

---

Richard H. Spady, *Freight Transport Regulation: Equity, Efficiency, and Competition in the Rail and Trucking Industries* (MIT Press, 1981); and Donald J. Harmatuck, "A Policy-Sensitive Railway Cost Function," *Logistics and Transportation Review*, vol. 15 (May 1979), pp. 277–315.

15. Friedlaender and Spady, *Freight Transport Regulation*, app. B.

16. This result comes from applying mean values for gross ton-miles of passenger and freight services and track-mileage for all Class I railroads as of 1969 to the following formula from Keeler, "Railroad Costs": mean value of ton-miles of freight service was 25.06 billion, mean value of gross ton-miles of passenger service was 1.09 billion, and mean track size was 4,807 miles. The formula for percent of costs variable is as shown in Keeler, "Railroad Costs," p. 207, evaluated at the mean values listed above, which come from Interstate Commerce Commission, *Transport Statistics—Year Ending December 31, 1969*, vol. 1: *Railroads* (Government Printing Office, 1970).

17. Harris, "Rationalizing the Rail Freight Industry," pp. 64–65.

route-mile, only 90 percent of costs are variable with the Harris specification. The Harmatuck study, like the Harris and Keeler studies, generates very high traffic densities. Minimum efficient density in his results appear to be more than twenty times the mean density of about 3,000 net ton-miles per route-mile.[18] However, Friedlaender and Spady have said that such estimates of minimum efficient density are likely to be extrapolations beyond the data sample. The important thing about the Harmatuck cost function is that it flattens out at relatively low densities. At twice the mean traffic density (or about 7 million net ton-miles per route-mile), fully 97.5 percent of costs are variable.[19] Thus the very high minimum efficient densities implicit in Harmatuck's results are probably artifacts of his specification. For practical purposes, his cost curve flattens out at 7 million to 10 million net ton-miles per route-mile. Harmatuck's estimated percentages of costs variable are very much in line with those of Harris and Keeler: specifically, he finds a percent of costs variable of 53 percent for a typical route-mile in 1969.[20]

Since Caves, Christensen, and Swanson do not explicitly introduce route-mileage or track-mileage into their equations, it is not possible to get an estimate of minimum efficient traffic density from their model. But it would be most nearly consistent with those of Harmatuck, Harris, and Keeler discussed so far, with route-mileage held constant. The results of Caves, Christensen, and Swanson are consistent with those of the other studies in that they show cost elasticities of slightly over 60 percent in the 1950s and 1960s. Their higher cost elasticity for the mid-1970s of just over 70 percent is consistent with the rise in traffic densities that occurred in the 1970s, as documented in tables 3-2 and 3-3.[21]

Friedlaender and Spady's study is perhaps the most sophisticated of those analyzed so far because it attempts to use the most generalized technology and to analyze separately the effects of way-and-structures capital and route-mileage on railroad costs. Their estimate of minimum efficient density is one of the lower ones—8.2 million net ton-miles per route-mile—though it is roughly consistent with Harmatuck's results as interpreted here.[22]

18. Harmatuck, "A Policy-Sensitive Railway Cost Function," p. 296.

19. Ibid., p. 304.

20. Ibid., p. 299.

21. Caves, Christensen, and Swanson, "Productivity Growth," p. 998.

22. The minimum efficient density implicit in Friedlaender and Spady's results can be calculated as follows. The mean ton-mileage for a firm in their sample is 24,086 million and

On the other hand, Friedlaender and Spady's estimate of the mean percent of costs variable at first seems to be out of line with the others— they found it to be 89.5 percent for an average firm.[23] But close analysis indicates that their results are in fact quite consistent with the other studies, for their estimate of 89.5 percent of costs variable is based on a much higher mean traffic density than is used in any of the other studies. Through the use of a dummy variable, Friedlaender and Spady specify their cost function so that costs fall sharply and discretely at 1 million gross ton-miles per route-mile.[24] Their study was thus not intended to measure percent of costs variable at very low traffic densities, because the cost curve is likely to fall smoothly around 1 million gross ton-miles per route-mile rather than abruptly, so that the real cost curve will not be nearly so flat around that point as their results imply, and marginal costs would be much further below average costs.

Instead, Friedlaender and Spady's estimated percent of costs variable should be taken as applying at the mean traffic density for main-line routes having traffic densities *above* 1 million gross ton-miles per route-mile. Since over 25 percent of the nation's route-mileage carries under 1 million tons a year, the mean density for these higher-density routes should be substantially above Friedlaender and Spady's sample mean of 3.56 million. This result is quite consistent with a cost function that flattens out completely around 8 million to 10 million net ton-miles per route-mile. In this sense, Friedlaender and Spady's results appear to be consistent with those of the other studies, which found much lower percentages of costs variable based on the inclusion of many miles of low-density branch lines.

In addition to estimating returns to traffic density, several of the studies, including those of Caves, Christensen, and Swanson and of Keeler, estimated returns to firm size. In no case was it possible to reject the hypothesis of constant returns to firm size, but Caves, Christensen,

---

the mean route-mileage is 6,760.4 (*Freight Transport Regulation*, p. 237). The mean route density overall is therefore 24,086/6,760.4 = 3.56 million net ton-miles per route-mile. To achieve minimum efficient scale for an average-size firm, Friedlaender and Spady state that the firm would have to increase its freight traffic by a factor of 2.3 (p. 156), so that the minimum efficient density is 2.3 × 3.56 = 8.2 million. And this understates the minimum efficient density somewhat for a freight-service-only line, because the average firm under consideration carries some passenger traffic.

23. Ibid., p. 157.
24. Ibid., app. B.

and Swanson found mildly increasing returns, Friedlaender and Spady found evidence of decreasing returns, or managerial diseconomies, and I found constant returns.[25]

All the studies mentioned so far are based on cross sectional or pooled cross section and time series analysis of relatively large, Class I railroads, with annual revenues of over $5 million before 1975 and over $10 million after 1975. Several other studies have been done based on samples of smaller, Class II and Class III railroads (sometimes called short lines), which usually have both shorter hauls and higher densities than Class I carriers.

One of these studies, by Sidhu, Charney, and Due, is a cross sectional study, much akin to those by Harris and Miller, aimed at finding long-run economies of density and length of haul for Class II railroads.[26] As in the case of studies for larger railroads, Sidhu, Charney, and Due found substantial economies of density, with a cost elasticity of 0.67 for a median firm and a route-density of 136,000 net ton-miles per route-mile. On the other hand, they found very low minimum efficient density of not much over 1.3 million net ton-miles per route-mile, far lower than the minimum efficient densities found in studies of Class I roads. This discrepancy is probably due to the different technology connected with the very short hauls involved in Class II railroading—specifically, the median length of haul in the sample of Sidhu and others was only 14 miles, though in Class I samples length of haul is typically over 300 miles. Such short hauls are likely to entail much more switching and terminal operation, with the result that shorter trains are more practical than the longer trains used in main-line railroading. But this conclusion is speculative. And indeed, time series studies of short-line railroads (which admittedly should yield short-run as opposed to long-run estimates of cost elasticities) give rather different results. Thus a time series analysis of ten Class II railroads by Charney, Sidhu, and Due found much lower short-run cost elasticities, with six out of the ten firms displaying elasticities below 0.3, and all of them well below one.[27]

25. Caves, Christensen, and Swanson, "Productivity Growth," p. 999; Friedlaender and Spady, *Freight Transport Regulation*, p. 163; and Keeler, "Railroad Costs."

26. Nancy D. Sidhu, Alberta Charney, and John F. Due, "Cost Functions of Class II Railroads and the Viability of Light Traffic Density Railway Lines," *Quarterly Review of Economics and Business*, vol. 17 (Autumn 1977), pp. 7–24; Harris, "Economies of Density"; and Miller, "Economies of Scale in Railroading."

27. Alberta H. Charney, Nancy D. Sidhu, and John F. Due, "Short Run Cost Functions for Class II Railroads," *Logistics and Transportation Review*, vol. 13 (December 1977), pp. 345–59.

This picture of short-run costs for short lines is further confirmed by two recent and highly sophisticated studies of short-line roads, one by Braeutigam, Daughety, and Turnquist, the other by Jara-Diaz and Winston.[28] Both studies are based on highly disaggregated data collected confidentially from small railroads with simple route structures, to minimize aggregation errors. Furthermore, in different ways, each study reaches a new level of sophistication in the estimation of railroad costs, albeit for specialized circumstances.

The study by Braeutigam and others blends a priori engineering evidence with a translog econometric specification, and it is innovative because it incorporates speed, in both line-haul and yard operations, into its specification. Although the authors do not state the specific route density, length of haul, or size of their sample firm, they do state that it is a small bridge line with a simple route structure. It is thus interesting to note that they find a cost elasticity of only 0.17 for this firm. Since it is a short-run cost elasticity, with both way-and-structures capital and route-mileage held constant, their result is not directly comparable with the results of studies for Class I railroads. Nevertheless, their result is within the range found for similar roads by Sidhu, Charney, and Due in time series. Since it is based on data from a bridge-line railroad without many terminal operations, it is also consistent with the notion that some short-line railroads fail to exhibit strong economies of density because of a prevalence of terminal operations.

The study by Jara-Diaz and Winston is also based on time series analysis of very small short-line railroads. Its most important innovations are level of disaggregation down to individual freight hauls (as explained in chapter 3 above) and specification so as to test the hypothesis of multiproduct natural monopoly (also described in chapter 3). The two firms in the Jara-Diaz and Winston sample are relatively high-density short-haul lines, bulk commodities making up most of their traffic.

For the first firm in their sample, with a route density of 8 million to 9 million net ton-miles per route-mile, Jara-Diaz and Winston find 35 percent of costs variable. For the second, with a route density of over 11 million net ton-miles per route-mile for half of its length and about 5 million for the rest, the overall cost elasticity is 0.79. Again, because

28. Ronald R. Braeutigam, Andrew F. Daughety, and Mark A. Turnquist, "The Estimation of Hybrid Cost Functions for a Railroad Firm," *Review of Economics and Statistics,* vol. 64 (August 1982), pp. 394–404; and Sergio Jara-Diaz and Clifford Winston, "Multiproduct Transportation Cost Functions: Scale and Scope in Railroad Operations," April 1981.

these are short-run cost elasticities, only with caution should they be compared with others summarized here. But it is worth noting that they are consistently below one and that they only approach one as densities get quite high.

The results of this analysis of rail cost studies were summarized in tables 3-1 and 3-4 and warrant several important conclusions. First, most of the nation's rail system operates subject to increasing returns to scale and has elements of natural monopoly, whether considered in a single-product or a multiproduct setting. Second, at some point between 8 million and 15 million or more net ton-miles per route-mile, depending on commodity mix, the cost curve for Class I railroads flattens out and a large part of the traffic in the system flows over this flat part. Third, for very short-haul, terminal-oriented railroads, the long-run cost curve seems to flatten out much sooner (say, at under 2 million net ton-miles per route-mile). Even here, however, there seems to be an exception: short-haul routes specializing in bridge operations and bulk commodities and not requiring extensive switching are much more akin to main-line railroads in their economies of density. Fourth, there are considerable economies of longer hauls. Fifth, there are constant or mildly decreasing returns to larger firm sizes, when route density is held constant. Finally, although the railroad industry is one of the most intensively studied of all industries by econometricians, there is still much to learn about the structure of railroad costs.

Mathematical Development
of Theories of Regulation

THE simplest models are based on the problems of optimal differential pricing among different groups of consumers (producer payoffs are ignored for the time being). Suppose that a regulator in a certain group of markets is able to control the prices of n commodities or services, produced in quantities $Q_1, \ldots, Q_n$, and that he is aware of the producer's total cost function:

$$TC = TC(Q_1, \ldots Q_n),$$

which may well be subject to scale economies, that is, marginal cost pricing on all commodities may not recover total costs. He is also aware of each of the independent demand functions:

(1) $$P_i = P_i(Q_1), \qquad i = 1, \ldots, n,$$

where P_i is the price charged for good i. Finally (and at the heart of a Chicago-type regulation model), he is aware of the marginal support available from a unit of consumer surplus in each market:

(2) $$S = S(CS_1, \ldots, CS_n),$$

where

(3) $$CS_i = \int_0^Q iP_i(Q_i)\, dQ_i - P_iQ_i.$$

This model is in fact identical to that of Peltzman, who also bases political support on consumer surplus.[1] But he does not explicitly introduce

1. Sam Peltzman, "Toward a More General Theory of Regulation," *Journal of Law and Economics*, vol. 19 (August 1976), pp. 211–44.

demand functions into his analysis, and he specifically assumes no scale economies.

The Ramsey problem is then to set prices so as to maximize net social benefits, defined as the total area under all demand curves minus total cost, subject to a break-even constraint. The Lagrangean expression is

(4)
$$L = \sum_{1}^{n} \int_{0}^{Q_i} P_i(Q_i) \, dQ_i - TC(Q_i, \ldots, Q_n)$$
$$+ \lambda \left[\sum_{1}^{n} (P_i Q_i - TC) \right],$$

where λ is the Lagrange multiplier. The first-order conditions for a maximum are

(5)
$$P_i - \frac{\partial TC}{\partial Q_i} + \lambda(P_i + Q_i) \frac{dP_i}{dQ_i} - \frac{\partial TC}{\partial Q_i} = 0, \qquad i = 1, \ldots, n,$$

and

(6)
$$\sum_{1}^{n} P_i Q_i - TC = 0.$$

The relation between price and marginal cost can then be rewritten as

(7)
$$\frac{1}{(1 + \lambda)\epsilon} = \frac{P_i - MC_i}{P_i}, \qquad i = 1, \ldots, n,$$

where ϵ_i is the demand elasticity for good i and MC_i is its marginal cost

The Peltzman problem, on the other hand, entails maximization of political support subject to a break-even constraint, so the Lagrangean expression is

(8)
$$M = S(CS_1, \ldots, CS_n) + \mu[P_n Q_n - TC(Q_1, \ldots, Q_n)],$$

where CS is as defined above and μ is the Lagrange multiplier. Conditions for the maximum, in addition to the break-even constraint, are

(9)
$$\frac{S_i(Q_i dP_i)}{dQ_i} + \mu(P_i) + \frac{Q_i k P_i}{dQ_i} - \frac{\partial TC}{\partial Q_i} = 0, \qquad i = 1, \ldots, n,$$

where S_i is equal to the marginal political support generated by an extra unit of consumer surplus made available from consumption of commodity i. This can be rewritten:

(10) $$\frac{\mu - S_i}{\mu}\left(\frac{1}{\epsilon_i}\right) = \frac{P_i - MC_i}{P_i}, \qquad i = 1, \ldots, n,$$

where once again ϵ_i is the demand elasticity for good i at the equilibrium point.[2]

To interpret this condition, note first that the Lagrange multiplier μ is the marginal political support generated by an extra dollar's subsidy (arriving as a windfall) available to the regulator. On the other hand, S_i is the marginal political support available from an extra dollar's worth of consumer surplus for good i.

If a dollar's worth of consumer surplus on the margin generates the same amount of political support for all goods, the Peltzman model turns into the Ramsey model, which in turn becomes the first-best model with constant returns to scale. Whereas prices will be inversely correlated with demand elasticities in the Ramsey model (as in the monopoly model), they will generally not be so correlated in the Peltzman model. The only exception to this occurs when the political support of a dollar's worth of consumer surplus is itself inversely related to the demand elasticity across groups. Thus if prices are not inversely related to the demand elasticities, there is adequate reason to reject the Ramsey model in favor of the Peltzman model, although failure to find such a correlation does not necessarily allow one to reject the Peltzman model. (Nevertheless, if such an inverse correlation were observed in a given set of regulated markets, a believer in the Peltzman model would have to give a persuasive reason for the model's result.)

Also, price can be below marginal cost in the Peltzman model (as originally indicated by Peltzman) provided that the marginal political support from a dollar's worth of consumption surplus exceeds the marginal political support of a dollar's worth of subsidy income. Whereas in the Ramsey subcase the regulator enhances efficiency to increase support, in this case the regulator sacrifices it to achieve that goal (as originally pointed out by Peltzman).

An important point to emerge from this is that a maximizer of political support can improve economic efficiency or harm it through the regula-

2. A result very similar to this one was independently derived by Thomas Ross, "Determining Regulators' Social Welfare Weights," November 1980. I became aware of this only after I had presented the same result at the University of Chicago's Industrial Organization Workshop in January 1981. Ross, however, based his result on a social welfare function rather than a political support function, and did not see that this result linked the Chicago and second-best theories.

tory process. Ultimately this depends on the extent to which political support is concentrated among users of particular goods or services, making inefficient transfers attractive. Given the levels of political support afforded by each group, it can be argued that the regulators do indeed maximize efficiency in this sense. This is evidently what Becker meant in his comment on Peltzman's work.[3]

A broad conclusion on the empirical validity of various theories of regulation stems from this analysis. A number of observers of regulation believe that a good theory of regulation should be able to predict when an industry will be regulated and when it will not. Like Posner, they have therefore been puzzled by the fact that some regulated industries (such as agriculture and trucking) are naturally competitive, and regulation appears to reduce efficiency by transferring income.[4] On the other hand, other industries bear some resemblance to natural monopolies, and the tendency of regulators to hold prices down or cross-subsidize bears more resemblance to public interest or second-best regulation. The foregoing analysis shows clearly that both scale economies and coalitions of voters matter to a support-maximizing regulator, who, with increasing returns, could behave remarkably like a public-interest regulator. In that sense, the support-maximizing and public-interest theories of regulation are not mutually exclusive in the way many writers have suggested that they somehow must be, and it should not be surprising that in some industries one explanation could dominate, and in other industries, another explanation could.

To make the model more relevant to the railroad industry, I extend it in a direction not previously taken in either the second-best or the Chicago model: I explicitly include service-extensiveness as part of the model. In most transportation and communications industries, there are political and social benefits in extending services into low-density regions. Furthermore, because at low densities some modes of transportation and communication are subject to increasing returns to traffic density, the cost of serving low-density routes is higher than the cost of serving high-density routes. If the system size is at all variable, the regulator will attempt to optimize political support by keeping a system in service, as well as optimizing through prices. Throughout the nation

3. Gary Becker, "Comment," *Journal of Law and Economics*, vol. 19 (August 1976), pp. 245–48.
4. Richard A. Posner, "Theories of Economic Regulation," *Bell Journal of Economics*, vol. 5 (Autumn 1974), pp. 335–58.

benefit to each group of consumers (shippers) is assumed to be a function not only of quantity of service purchased, but also of the route network available, with consumer surplus increasing with an increase in system size, all other things being equal. Diminishing marginal benefits of system size can be assumed if the trackage is implicitly ordered so that if mileage is cut the least economic is abandoned first, and so forth. With these assumptions, the demand for rail service in the nation will take the form:

$$(11) \qquad\qquad P_i = P_i(Q_i, T)$$

for each commodity, where T is route-miles available in the national rail system, and the other variables are as defined above.

For this model route-miles will also enter the cost function. Specifically, the total cost function is assumed to be

$$(12) \qquad\qquad TC = TC(Q_i, \ldots, Q_n, T),$$

where $\partial TC/\partial T > 0$. This assumption is sufficient to guarantee increasing returns to traffic density for a given route, because if there were constant returns, it would be costless to spread traffic out among as many routes as desired, and

$$\frac{\partial TC}{\partial T} = 0.$$

As before, the conditions are separately set for both the Ramsey-pricing and the Peltzman-pricing regulators. The Lagrangean expression for the Ramsey pricer is

$$(13) \qquad L = \sum_1^n \int_0^{Q_i} P_i(Q_i, T) \, dQ_i - TC + \lambda \left(\sum_1^n P_i Q_i - TC \right).$$

This generates optimal first-order conditions including the constraint, a set of price-cost relationships identical in apperance to equation 5 above, and the following relationship for the benefits and costs of route expansion:

$$(14) \qquad \sum_1^n \int_0^{Q_i} \frac{\partial P_i}{\partial T} = \frac{\partial TC}{\partial T} - \lambda \left(\sum_1^n \frac{\partial P_i}{\partial TQ_i} \frac{\partial TC}{\partial T} \right).$$

Basically this condition states that the regulator will require continuation of service on routes to the point at which the marginal social benefit of providing the service equals the marginal shadow price of providing it. If there were no revenue constraint—that is, if subsidy were possible—service would be subsidized and provided to the point where the marginal social benefit of an extra route-mile equaled the marginal cost. That condition would hold if λ were 0. Since cross-subsidy money is costlier to the Ramsey pricer than direct subsidy money is to the first-best regulator, one would expect the optimal second-best to be smaller than the optimal first-best system.

The political-support-maximizing regulator will, as before, maximize consumer surplus subject to a break-even constraint. His problem can be characterized by the Lagrangean expression:

$$(15) \quad M = S(CS_1, \ldots, CS_n) + \mu \left[\sum_1^n P_i Q_i - TC(Q_i, \ldots, Q_n, T) \right],$$

where

$$CS_i = \int_0^{Q_i} P_i(Q_i, T) \, dQ_i - P_i Q_i, \text{ and } i = 1, \ldots, n.$$

Once again, all but one of the first-order conditions look like those of the earlier problem. The one that differs is

$$(16) \quad \sum_1^n S_i \left[\int_0^{Q_i} \left(\frac{\partial P_i(Q_i T)}{\partial T} \right) dQ_i - Q_i \frac{\partial P_i}{\partial T} \right] = -\mu \left(\sum_1^n \frac{\partial P_i}{\partial T} Q_i - \frac{\partial TC}{\partial T} \right).$$

It too has a straightforward intuitive meaning: it indicates that the regulator will require service to the point at which the marginal political support gained from providing an extra unit of service (the left-hand side of the equation) equals the marginal amount lost from higher prices necessary to cross-subsidize the service (the right-hand side).

Once again, the political-support maximizer will behave equivalently to the second-best pricer provided that the marginal political support of a unit of consumer surplus from each consumer group is the same for all groups. (Note that for $S_i \equiv 1$ and $\mu = \lambda + 1$, the second-best and support-maximizing conditions are equivalent.)

What are the implications of the political-support-maximizing theory relative to the second-best theory for the provision of low-density service? Although it is not obvious from the formulas alone, use of them alongside some crude empirical inferences can certainly suggest a hypothesis: the benefits of service to small communities are concentrated among fewer people than are the costs of taxing the users of higher-density routes to cross-subsidize such service. Hence residents of small communities will engage in "boosterism"—political lobbying for implicitly subsidized service to their communities—and a support-maximizing regulator will provide more low-density service than a benefit-cost analysis could justify.

A Model with Factor Payoffs and Deficits

THE MODEL developed in chapter 4 and applied to the railroad industry is unrealistic in a number of ways—two in particular. First, it ignores the benefits that rail labor receives from public intervention in the industry. Second, it assumes that a break-even constraint applies, when in fact the industry has run chronic deficits in opportunity costs, and significant parts of it now receive direct government subsidies. To take account of these facts, the model is now further generalized and suggestions made on how rail reform could be treated as a comparative statics problem with such a model, albeit an extremely difficult one to solve.

To take account of potential political gains from labor payoffs, it is assumed that the wage rate enters the political support function directly, so that an increase in the wage rate increases political support, other aspects of service being held constant. Increases in service (that is, ton-miles handled) or routes served will in all likelihood increase labor support as well, just as labor tends to protest the discontinuation of uneconomic service. Because these variables enter the support function in ways other than through consumer surplus once organized labor support is admitted, consumer surplus is dropped from notation in the support function, as Peltzman originally did.

The existence of railroad deficits can be taken account of in the support function as well. That is, if a government must subsidize rail service, the lost taxpayer dollars cost political support. For this analysis, the index of commodities hauled is also simplified, so that all tonnage can be lumped together in a single quantity Q with rate P. Also, demand is made a function of price rather than quantity.

Based on these assumptions, the public authority will maximize the support function:

(1) $$S = S(P, T, W, D),$$

subject to the constraint that

(2) $$D = TC[Q(P, T), W, T] - PQ(P, T),$$

where D is the deficit. The Lagrangean expression is then

(3) $$M = S(P, T, W, D) + \lambda(D - TC + PQ).$$

The first-order conditions are:

(4) $$\frac{\partial M}{\partial P} = \frac{\partial S}{\partial P} - \lambda\left(Q + P\frac{\partial Q}{\partial P}\right) = 0;$$

(5) $$\frac{\partial M}{\partial T} = \frac{\partial S}{\partial T} - \lambda\left(\frac{\partial TC}{\partial Q}\frac{\partial Q}{\partial T}\right) - \lambda\frac{\partial TC}{\partial T} + \lambda P\frac{\partial Q}{\partial T} = 0;$$

(6) $$\frac{\partial M}{\partial W} = \frac{\partial S}{\partial W} - \lambda\frac{\partial TC}{\partial W} = 0;$$

and

(7) $$\frac{\partial M}{\partial D} = \frac{\partial S}{\partial D} + \lambda = 0;$$

plus the constant.

These conditions indicate, sensibly, that the marginal support to be gained from a taxpayer's dollar (equal to the Lagrange multiplier) should be equal in all uses. This includes the fact that a dollar spent reducing the deficit should have the same impact as a dollar spent subsidizing various dimensions of service to gain support.

The need for regulatory change in the railroad industry can easily be set up (if not solved) as a comparative-statics problem based on these first-order conditions. For example, as the rail plant wears out and impoverished railroads run out of cash, more government subsidy money is needed to keep service going. This can be viewed as a parametric increase in the cost function from the government's viewpoint. One could thus imagine multiplying the total cost function in the above conditions by a parameter, α, starting with $\alpha = 1$ and then allowing it to increase slightly. This would generate a comparative-statics problem much like those worked out by Peltzman, wherein one could analyze the effect of the shift in costs on wages paid, prices charged, size of the route system, and the deficit level.

Analytically, this problem is intractable because the Lagrangean expression contains ambiguous cross-partial derivatives that make it difficult to place a priori restrictions on the effects of deregulation. Among the various possible outcomes, however, one stands out as most consistent with the evidence so far. Just as a consumer, faced with a cut in income, is likely to spread the effects of the cut by reducing consumption of a number of goods, the political system is likely to spread out the costs of the change, so that some route-mileage would be abandoned, rates would go up, wages would decline somewhat (or there would be some work-rule reform), and subsidies would increase (as long as the support function was stable, of course—election of a budget-cutting administration and Congress could be a shift in the function).

In fact, as the rail situation has deteriorated, all these things have occurred. When Conrail was formed, for instance, some formerly private lines were abandoned, and some that would have been abandoned were converted to short lines not subject to union wages or work rules. Government subsidies have increased and now include a number of midwestern routes as well as eastern ones. Finally, some well-publicized and fought-over provisions of recent rail regulatory reform acts allow for increases in rates, although conflict continues about just how large such increases may legally be.

While this explanation of the rail regulatory reform process is neither rigorous nor descriptively complete, it does indicate how a large part of the current change in government policy toward the railroad industry is at least consistent with a political-support-maximization model.

Index

177